Help Club for Moms

Moms encouraging moms to know the love of Christ

Holidays with the Help Club

Holidays with the Help Club

This book takes you from November – January

Designed by Kristall Willis   www.kwdesignsco.com

Holidays with the Help Club

"Let your light shine before men in such a way that they may see your good works, and glorify your Father who is in Heaven." (Matthew 5:16)

Sweet Mom,

As we write this book, our hearts are burdened for how hard you work, especially during the holiday season. You wear so many hats and are charged with the task of juggling endless activities that don't slow down this time of year—they actually speed up! All of this can make you feel overwhelmed, drained, and even burned out at the end of it all. Just thinking about all of the tasks that need to be accomplished can make a mama feel weary. We are praying for this year to be different, and asking God to help you enjoy your Thanksgiving, Christmas, and New Year like never before.

We pray for this season to feel refreshing and uplifting as you approach each holiday with a more Christ-centered focus. The only way that we know how to have this type of focus is to spend time with Jesus. He directs our paths and lights our way. He brings peace to the weariness of our souls and gives us JOY in the midst of trials, unwanted circumstances, and endless tasks. He fills us up with new ways to love our "people" and bring others into His presence! Our prayer is that this season we will cling to that truth and allow Him to give us His vision for what He wants our holidays to look like.

This book is filled to the brim with practical ideas to help make your holidays meaningful and focused on Jesus. You will find organizational pieces that are intended to help you stress less about all the fuss so that you can spend more time with your children. There are activities, faith-filled ideas, and "Mom Tips" designed to help draw you closer to Jesus as a family! Most of all, this book is threaded throughout with words of hope and encouragement, reminding us of the gentle mercies of Jesus.

There are four essential components to this devotional workbook, designed to help you have a wonderful, Christ-centered Christmas: Prayer, Bible Study, *Mom Tips*, and *The Best Holiday Season Ever Organizational Planner*.

- **Prayer:** We believe prayer changes everything, and we encourage you to prayerfully consider finding someone who you can pray with once a week over the phone, preferably someone who is doing this Bible study as well. Even though we are all super busy during the holidays, this one habit of praying with a prayer partner helps you stay anchored to Christ during the hustle and bustle of the holiday season.

- **Bible Study:** Included in your workbook each week are three Bible studies (you choose which days to complete them). They begin with Scriptures to read and meditate on as well as an invitation to pray and fellowship with your beautiful Savior. The studies always end with "Questions to Ponder" and a "Faith-Filled Idea." These are meant to stir your heart and mind into action, and bring lasting, godly change into your everyday life! We pray the Holy Spirit draws you into a deeper relationship with your Heavenly Father as you actively endeavor to know Him more.

- **Mom Tips:** We are so excited to share our "Mom Tips" with you each week! These practical ideas are holiday-specific, and meant to enhance your life and role as a Christian wife, mom, homemaker, and friend. You can pray about which tips to try and check them off as you accomplish them. Completing them all or doing only one is just fine!

- *The Best Holiday Season Ever Organizational Planner*: Do you long for a more organized holiday season? Do you need a little help with planning your holidays so you can have time to do fun and meaningful activities with your kids? You are going to LOVE our new *Best Holiday Season Ever Organizational Planner*. All you do is print out the planner, grab a cup of something delicious, and go to your favorite spot where you can pray and plan. This planner will help you think through your Thanksgiving, Christmas, and New Year in a more organized and thoughtful way, so you can have less stress and more fun memories with your family.

Our prayer is that, with the divine help of the Holy Spirit, and with some tips from other seasoned moms who have walked this path many times, we will be able to spend time on what truly matters this holiday season—heart-changing time with Jesus, precious time with our children, making lasting memories with our families, and drawing people closer to Jesus!

Blessings and love,

The Help Club for Moms Team

P.S. – We would love to bless you by gifting several exclusive FREE printables to you! Thank you for supporting the Help Club for Moms; we are so very blessed by you! **Check out www.myhelpclubformoms.com to access these printables.**

Table of Contents

Table of Contents

Holidays with the Help Club

Best Holiday Season Ever!

Organizational Planner

Let Christ Make Your Home

❧ Diverse Perspectives From Two Seasoned Moms ❧

Dear Precious Child of God,

As the holidays approach, how are you feeling? Are you excited to see friends and family all together, but dread the pressure to clean, cook, and decorate like Joanna Gaines? Would you like to celebrate special holiday moments with your family and friends, free of stress?

We welcome you to join us for a holiday season like no other—where you partner with Jesus and prayerfully plan and organize your Thanksgiving, Christmas, and New Year's in such a way that you work smarter, not harder, so you can celebrate along with your family. In *The Best Holiday Season Ever Organizational Planner*, we provide tried-and-true ideas that can make your workload easier to manage. A mom in tune with the Holy Spirit can set a joyful, relaxed tone at home that nurtures the connections that matter most, because she is at peace.

Friend, there is no cookie-cutter Christian formula for every mom to follow. We'd like you to meet Melissa and Rachel, who are seasoned moms with grown children, and who come from two very different backgrounds. They have a heart to share practical wisdom, gleaned from years of homemaking, with the next generation. They share their stories with you to demonstrate that it matters less where your story began and more where you are going in your life with Christ (Romans 6:4).

As early as I can remember, I (Melissa) had the privilege of a happy, Christian home, and a mother who modeled how to be an efficient homemaker and gracious hostess. My mom's enthusiasm for keeping a tidy, well-organized, comfortable, welcoming haven for our friends and family rubbed off on me. Even with a part-time job, she prioritized maintaining an impeccable space and warm heart. My mom loved entertaining and planning themed parties, birthdays, and holidays that were very festive and fun. She put her heart and soul into making beautiful memories. My experience was pleasant and memorable. By the time I had a home and family of my own, I had adopted her homemaking habits and skills to care for my family and friends, and to carry on treasured traditions that were lovingly passed down to me.

My (Rachel's) childhood was a bit more complicated. My younger years were filled with warm holiday memories of a loving, supportive mother of four girls who decorated the live Christmas tree, baked cookies, pies, and Baby Jesus' Birthday Cake, took us to Christmas Eve Candlelight Service and Easter Sunrise Celebration, made old family recipes for Thanksgiving Dinner, and scrambled her brood to the Fourth of July parade to wave flags and honor Veterans. However, by time I was seven years old everything changed.

On the outside, Mom seemed positive and happy, but it covered a deep sadness that drew her into alcohol abuse. Her alcoholism was disrupting every aspect of our family life; home became chaotic and frightening. When my dad traveled for business, which was often, my mom binge-drank, leaving my siblings and me to fend for ourselves. Then, when I was 15 years old—only a year old in the Lord—my father died. Without his restraining presence, Mom could not cope. I became a "foster kid," living in several homes during my high school years. Fortunately, my foster families were decent, caring people—some were Christians—who gave me a taste of "normal" family life and inspired hope in me. My foster moms had hearts to serve, and I am grateful I experienced their "mothering" as a healthy model of caring for a home and children. Living with these women encouraged me to want to have a Christian home of my own.

Do you resonate with either of these life stories? Your upbringing can definitely play a large part in how you feel about holidays. Many of you dear ones have other reasons for feeling overwhelmed by the season. You may have circumstances in your life that cause you to need to establish your own set of priorities. Your child may suffer from chronic health issues or special needs, or perhaps you are caring for one or both of your aging parents. No matter the circumstances of your life at this moment, or the home that you grew up in, beginning today, as surely as the Lord lives in you, you can learn to identify and develop your unique holiday priorities. With the Lord's help and the encouragement found in these pages, you'll be inspired to better manage your holiday, pass on family traditions, and create wonderful, Christ-centered memories.

In *The Best Holiday Season Ever Organizational Planner*, we share tips and strategies to minimize stress and maximize your joy. Experiment with new habits and implement those suggestions to help make your holiday experiences more peaceful and rich. As always in the Help Club, we say "You do You!" We want you to do whatever works best for your family and your present set of circumstances. Prayerfully seek God's will for wisdom and discernment on how to make this planner work for you, your family, and your home. Complete all of it or pick and choose what you would like to use when. Go where God leads you. He loves you so much and has a perfect plan for your holiday organization, your family, and your beautiful heart as a woman!

Yours in joyful celebration,

Melissa Lain, Rachel Kindervater, and the Help Club for Moms Team

P.S. – **Check out www.myhelpclubformoms.com to access and download all the forms in this** *Planner*, **as well as other FREE printables!**

How to Use the
Best Holiday Season Ever!
Organizational Planner

"Therefore, my dear brothers and sisters, stand firm. Let nothing move you. Always give yourselves fully to the work of the Lord, because you know that your labor in the Lord is not in vain. " (1 Corinthians 15:58)

Are you struggling with the increasing pressures and demands that come this time of year? The expectations of others and ourselves to make holidays special can be overwhelming. Like walking on a treadmill that continues to get faster and steeper, you are left breathless, and wondering, "How do I get off?"

This planner is designed as a way for you to stop that treadmill of drivenness and demand, and step onto the peaceful path lit by God's Word (Psalm 119:105). With some planning and organization to manage the holidays, you can have more time and more fun with your family.

Enclosed in this planner are helpful checklists for Thanksgiving, Christmas, and New Year's. They provide many ideas to help you remember the little details of the season and to think ahead.

Also enclosed are many forms created to help you intentionally plan your holidays and break down the tasks into simple steps. Each form has easy-to-follow instructions to guide you as you plan. Imagine arriving at each special day ready to go with more joy and anticipation (and less stress) than you've ever experienced.

So, with this book, the downloadble printable forms from **www.myhelpclubformoms.com**, and a warm drink in hand, head for your favorite spot in your house and learn from seasoned moms who have created their own organized and festive homes for years while "seek(ing) first the kingdom of God and His righteousness" (Matthew 6:33).

One more thing, when you're done planning, be sure to grab a 3-ring binder to store all of your completed forms for handy reference. You could even send the blank forms to a copy center and have them spiral bound for easy accessibility. You will know what you need and where to locate it at all times.

We pray that using these resources will reinforce behaviors, build confidence, and establish habits that develop in you the character and commitment of our Lord Jesus Christ, who "...began a good work in you [and] will carry it on to completion..." (Philippians 1:6). He will help you create a Christ-centered Christmas for you and your family, that will bring Him glory for generations!

~ Plan Your Priorities ~

Here at the Help Club, our desire is to equip you to live purposefully by:
- **Knowing** your God-given priorities
- **Committing** yourself to those priorities
- **Planning** how to live out those priorities daily
- **Performing** them routinely until they become *your* priorities

What are "priorities" and why is everyone talking about "setting priorities?" Priorities are the important activities, practices, or relationships into which I put genuine effort and time because they define my purpose; the reason for which I was made. Setting priorities begins with knowing what really matters to my Creator and identifying how He wants me to participate in His story during my lifetime.

Priorities are foundational to building a strong spiritual home, one day at a time. These Biblical directives align a family's purpose with those of God's Kingdom. Having these "non-negotiables" may seem inflexible, but they give you the confidence to know when to say, "No" or "Yes." You are liberated from demands when you know your purpose and priorities. People-pleasing is often misunderstood as a virtue. However, God honors our obedience to Him.

The following acronym, based on material from the ministry of *Revive Our Hearts* by Nancy Leigh DeMoss, is a simple way to begin to discover God's priorities for you, and to implement them as your own:

P – **Pray** for wisdom and submission to God's Word (James 1:5).

R – **Review** God's priorities (Titus 2:4-5).
https://www.openbible.info/topics/purpose_in_life

I – **Inventory** use of your time and resources. After charting these areas for a week, ask yourself, "What do my choices reveal about my priorities? How do they align with God's priorities above?" (1 Timothy 1:12).

O – **Order** your schedule by making choices based on God's priorities (Psalm 119:113).

R – **Resist** the temptation to deviate from God's priorities. The enemy uses people-pleasing and the "tyranny of the urgent" to take us off-purpose (Galatians 1:10, 5:13).

I – **Input** from others. Seek counsel and accountability from your husband, godly friends, counselor, support partner, prayer partner, and mentors (Proverbs 9:9).

T – **Time** stewardship. Spend the limited number of hours you are given in light of eternity. Do all to the glory of God (Ephesians 5:15-18).

I – **Identify** "time robbers." What saps your energy and robs your time? Watch for the "little foxes that spoil the vines" (Song of Solomon 2:15).

E – **Experience** this season fully. Be all there in this season of life. Weep, rejoice, and celebrate with all your heart. Be present, now (Psalm 90:12).

S – **Sabbaths**. Frequently take breaks to refresh, regain perspective, reflect, and prioritize. Ponder the shortness of life vs. eternity. Stay sensitive and surrendered to the Spirit. Trust God. Rest in the Lord (Matthew 11:28).

Elements
of the
~Organizational Planner~

Holiday Checklists

"If any of you lacks wisdom, you should ask God, who gives generously to all without finding fault, and it will be given to you." (James 1:5)

In the following pages you will find detailed checklists for Thanksgiving, Christmas, and New Year's to help you brainstorm the big and little tasks that come with each holiday. Don't be overwhelmed by these lists as they are meant to inspire you and encourage you to think ahead. Pray over each checklist and allow God to show you what needs to be done for your particular home and family puzzle. Remember, you do you!

~ Thanksgiving ~

- [ ] Create a family "Communication Station" displaying *Weekly Planner*, *Monthly Planners*, and school/holiday event flyers.
- [ ] Record events/times on *Monthly Planners* in your binder.
- [ ] Finalize holiday travel plans and reservations; add to planners.
- [ ] Discuss travel and overnight plans with guests or hosts.
- [ ] If hosting a meal or party, send invitations; include what to bring, if relevant.
- [ ] Inventory/prepare Thanksgiving table linens, china, flatware, etc.; create a shopping list.
- [ ] Place orders for food from the grocer, baker, etc.
- [ ] Purchase a frozen turkey or order a fresh one to be picked up 1-2 days prior to your preparation. This saves space in your freezer and refrigerator, as well as saving time.
- [ ] Schedule family photo session and plan wardrobe; create a shopping list, if needed.
- [ ] Schedule hair, mani/pedi, and facial appointments or personal time for self-care.
- [ ] Begin Christmas *Gift Giving* form with your husband.
- [ ] Check the gift closet for gifts purchased throughout the year.
- [ ] Set up crafting/wrapping station(s); create a shopping list.
- [ ] Combine all shopping lists; schedule shopping trip(s) on *Weekly Planner*.
- [ ] Confirm guests for Thanksgiving meal and overnight accommodations.
- [ ] Combine groceries, gifts, and sundries lists.
- [ ] Gather recipes and ideas for the holiday.

☐ Use the *Meal Planner* form to create your menu for extra meals to prepare for children and visiting guests during Thanksgiving break.

☐ Carve a pumpkin with a Thanksgiving theme.

☐ Decorate front entry, dining table, and mantle/hearth. If you have time, add seasonal touches to the kitchen, gathering room, and bathroom (scented candles/potpourri, hand towels, dried arrangements, throw blankets/pillows, etc.). Use the *Delighted to Decorate* form.

☐ Complete your seasonal decor by setting a date in your *Weekly Planner* and *Monthly Planner*.

☐ Install leaves in the table, prepare for extra chairs or tables, if needed.

☐ Purchase paper goods, linens, and plastic containers for guests to take home leftovers.

☐ Store prepared baked goods in the freezer, pantry or refrigerator to keep fresh until the designated event.

☐ Prepare seasonal treats and store in airtight bags or containers.

☐ Delegate, Delegate, Delegate! Have the family help in tasks to reduce stress.

☐ Set a budget for your holiday spending, use *Gift Giving* form.

☐ Pull food out of the freezer to thaw for serving.

☐ Groceries purchased.

☐ Foods are prepped, i.e., veggies chopped, dips made, etc.

☐ Serving pieces accounted for, i.e., platters, spoons, etc.

☐ If traveling, make arrangements for boarding your pets. If you're not traveling bathe your dog(s).

☐ Prepare for travel: car maintenance, suitcases prepared, etc.

☐ Clean off counters and store unnecessary items to utilize space for serving and preparation of food.

☐ Set the table.

☐ Plan for adequate sleeping arrangements for overnight guests, i.e., linens, pillows, blankets, etc.

☐ Prepare a basket of seasonal fruits or baked items to share with a homebound individual or a neighbor. Include the kids on this effort to bless someone through giving.

☐ Pack up all Thanksgiving/fall decor in clear boxes, print out labels from www.myhelpclubformoms.com to place on boxes designated for the appropriate season.

☐ Prepare for Christmas card photo.

☐ _____

☐ _____

☐ _____

☐ _____

☐ _____

Holiday Checklists

"Once in our world, a stable had something in it that was bigger than our whole world." ~ C.S. Lewis

~ Christmas ~

- [ ] Purchase stamps and mail Christmas cards.
- [ ] Pull Christmas boxes from storage.
- [ ] Decorate house using the "Direction of Focus" concept from *Cleaning Compass* and *Delighted to Decorate*. Repair items that are broken and throw away those damaged beyond repair.
- [ ] Plan meals using leftovers from Thanksgiving.
- [ ] Using *Gift Giving* form make your shopping list.
- [ ] Prepare a menu for Christmas gatherings for the month of December using the *Meal Planner*.
- [ ] Hang Christmas lights.
- [ ] While hanging outside lights clean out gutters.
- [ ] Before draping exterior lights in shrubs, trim shrubs, this conserves the number of lights needed.
- [ ] While decorating doorways, porches, and entryways, clean surfaces, lights, etc.
- [ ] Start your Advent traditions (refer to Christmas Week One for ideas, suggestions, and tips).
- [ ] Mail out-of-town gifts for guaranteed delivery.
- [ ] Continue your gift shopping using *Gift Giving* form.
- [ ] Finish decorating practicing the "Focus 15."
- [ ] Establish a basket or box with all gift wrapping supplies for the family to easily access.
- [ ] Wrap gifts as they are purchased.
- [ ] Track gift purchased and wrapped on *Gift Giving* form.
- [ ] Place all receipts in the designated envelope for easy retrieval, as recommended on the *Gift Giving* form.
- [ ] Wrap freshly baked items and store in the freezer.
- [ ] Make a note of traditions on the *Weekly Planner* and *Monthly Planner*.
- [ ] Add new additions for seasonal events and activities on *New Additions and Traditions* form.

☐ Take time to enjoy and savor the beauty of your Christmas decor.

☐ Maintain your habits in *Meal Planning* and *Cleaning Compass*.

☐ Prepare the clothing you desire the family to wear for Christmas events and activities.

☐ Plan meals by using items in freezer, fridge, and pantry to accommodate for space in preparation of additional holiday shopping.

☐ Take inventory on serving pieces and dinnerware.

☐ Have kid's craft table decorations for use during special holiday mealtimes.

☐ Go caroling and provide seasonal treats to individuals who are homebound or in a nursing home.

☐ Put away annual decor in Christmas boxes as you add Christmas decor. This keeps surfaces clean and clutter-free.

☐ Prepare the sleeping arrangements for overnight guests.

☐ Purchase a puzzle to have family and guests complete during the holiday.

☐ Have dinner around the Christmas tree one evening with only the tree lights on.

☐ Review and bask in all your accomplishments via *Gift Giving* form, *Meal Planner*, *Cleaning Compass*, etc.

☐ Prepare for travel: car maintenance, suitcases prepared, etc.

☐ Pull pre-prepared frozen meals and baked items from the freezer.

☐ Have kids help pack baked goodies in gift boxes for neighbors and public service workers.

☐ Purchase extra batteries for new gifts and misc.

☐ Clear surfaces for food preparation and serving, as well as for guests' personal belongings while they are visiting.

☐ Assign each child to purge old toys, books, and clothing in preparation for new items gifted while home from school on holiday break.

☐ Wipe down and sweep entryways, porches, and patios for refreshing welcome for guests.

☐ Final grocery run, pick up meat, poultry and other large staples for holiday meals.

☐ Set holiday table.

☐ Find time to rest, relax and bask in your preparations for this holiday season. Arise early with your favorite drink in hand. Turn on Christmas lights and enjoy the beauty of your home while reading your Help Club devotional.

☐ _____

☐ _____

☐ _____

☐ _____

"We cannot start over but we can begin now, and make a new beginning."
~ Zig Ziglar

∼ New Year's ∼

- ☐ Create a social media invitation for New Year's party.
- ☐ Buy party favors and fireworks.
- ☐ Cast photos of last years party on the TV or family favorite photos from previous year.
- ☐ Replace regular light bulbs with party bulbs.
- ☐ Provide props and a designated area for photo ops.
- ☐ Create a playlist for the theme of the party.
- ☐ Plan on games based on the theme for the party.
- ☐ Prepare a traditional New Year meal: cabbage, black eye peas, greens and cornbread (very southern).
- ☐ Create a time capsule (as mentioned on page 140).
- ☐ Have family and guests participate in the "Snapshot of my Year" (as mentioned on page 141).
- ☐ _____
- ☐ _____
- ☐ _____
- ☐ _____
- ☐ _____
- ☐ _____
- ☐ _____
- ☐ _____
- ☐ _____

Organizational Forms

Life Blueprint
Instruction Guide

"We continually ask God to fill you with the knowledge of his will through all the wisdom and understanding that the Spirit gives, so that you may live a life worthy of the Lord and please him in every way."
~ Colossians 1:9b-10a

The *Life Blueprint* is used as a quick reference for remaining grounded and confident in your commitments. God designed a woman to be an influencer in her home, church, community, and the world. This kind of leadership is essentially modeling desirable traits with an invitation for others to follow. But what guides her? The wise woman of God seeks the counsel of her husband, elders, God's Word, and the Holy Spirit. When she aligns with God's will she becomes a blueprint, a design for others to copy.

The *Life Blueprint* is a visual reminder of God's priorities on which to build our days and weeks and months and years. Refer to it daily. Refine it weekly to customize it for you and your family as you grow, and notice how to more closely follow the Designer's plan.

Step 1: **Pray.** Ask the Lord to direct you regarding the commitments on your *Life Blueprint*.

Step 2: **Spend about 15 minutes on Sunday in prayerful consideration,** seeking the Lord as you formulate your intentions for the week on the *Life Blueprint* form.

Step 3: **Fill in the date.**

Step 4: **Choose your theme or motivation verse.** Meditate on your chosen Scripture with the intent to be changed by it.

Step 5: What feelings of appreciation does your verse stir up in you? **Journal your thoughts in the "Gratitude" space.** As A.W. Tozer said, "Gratitude is an offering precious in the sight of God, and it is one that the poorest of us can make and be not poorer but richer for having made it."

Step 6: **The *Life Blueprint* lists six priorities:**

1. **Building Your Spirit** – Communing with God in His Word, prayer, meditation, and other spiritual disciplines. (See *Celebration of Discipline: The Path to Spiritual Growth* by Richard J. Foster)

2. **Respecting your Husband** – Placing your relationship with him above all others; showing him appreciation and commending him to your children throughout the day for those qualities and character traits to emulate. Presenting your physical and inner beauty.

3. **Loving your children** – Nurturing, training, and correcting them; enjoy them.

4. **Self Care** – Maintaining physical and emotional wellness; grooming and physical appearance; mental/intellectual development; social interaction; joy; and rest.

5. **Home Care** – Maintaining a clean, well-managed, safe, and welcoming environment for your family and guests.

6. **Commitments** – work; professional development and education; volunteering; caring for elderly relatives; home schooling research and preparation; children's activities, launching an adult child from home, etc.

NOTE: If any priorities encroach on others, pray with your husband to seek the Lord's guidance. Assess if your decisions are aligned with your family's mission. Are you being swayed by worldly or Christian cultural expectations? If so, then re-consider, re-evaluate, re-structure, or delegate. While some priorities will require more of your time than others, all are important.

REMEMBER: PRIORITIES ARE NON-NEGOTIABLES!

Step 7: **"Projects" are out-of-the-ordinary tasks with multiple steps to accomplish.** These household, personal, family, financial, professional, or health-related goals may take several days or weeks to complete. Select the next few steps to accomplish this week.

Step 8: **Write a brief prayer** for the Spirit of God to fill you with His perspective so that you love what He loves and want to keep the commitments of your *Life Blueprint*.

"Work willingly at whatever you do,
as though you were working for the Lord rather than for people."
~ Colossians 3:24 (NLT)

Notes

_____

_____

_____

_____

_____

_____

_____

_____

_____

_____

_____

Notes

Life Blueprint

Week of: _____

Theme/Motivation Verse:

> "   "

Gratitude:

Projects:

1.

2.

3.

Prayer:

Life Priorities:

1. Building my Spirit:

2. Respecting my Husband:

3. Loving my children:

4. Self Care:

5. Home Care:

6. Commitments:

Cleaning Compass
Instruction Guide

"Start by doing what is necessary; then do what's possible; then suddenly you are doing the impossible." ~ Francis of Assisi

The **Cleaning Compass** is a great tool to help you get your home ready for the holidays by easily tracking your "stem-to-stern" house cleaning. With this guide, will know what has been cleaned and when. This record gives you confidence that your house is "mostly" clean all the time. So instead of panicking when someone drops by unexpectedly or when you entertain this holiday season, you can greet your guest with a smile and no apologies!

And if you are too busy this month to finish everything in the *Cleaning Compass*, don't despair! You will have another chance next month. This plan is intended to bring you freedom, not enslave you. Go with the flow! Remember, you do you!

Between October and December, eliminate less urgent cleaning in some focus areas. Instead, for example, use the *Cleaning Compass* in the spare bedroom for dusting and sweeping to prepare the room for guests. Use the rest of your cleaning time to wash bed linens and make the bed. Additionally, think of ways to pamper your guest, like clearing dresser drawers so they can unpack, hanging a pumpkin-spice sachet in the closet, laying a cuddly fur throw blanket across the bed, and stacking books of interest on the nightstand.

Step 1: **Fill in the start date next to "Week of."**

Step 2: **"Direction of Focus."** Group all the rooms in your house into five cleaning spaces. Assign each cleaning space, called "Direction of Focus," to one week each month. This is an example of how to group cleaning spaces:
- Week 1: Kitchen
- Week 2: Public spaces – playroom, media room, deck/porch, entryways
- Week 3: Wet spaces – baths/laundry
- Week 4: Bedrooms
- Week 5: Extra spaces – attic, garage, seasonal tasks (washing exterior windows, pressure washing exterior surfaces, cleaning grill, etc.)

Step 3: **"Focus 15."** This highly effective practice requires a goal and a timer. The race begins! Can you finish the goal you set before the timer goes off? In your "Direction of Focus" for the week, write down tasks that can either be completed within 15 minutes, or one task that can be completed throughout the week by breaking it down into 15-minute segments. It is important to model good cleaning habits daily for your children, even for only 15 minutes. Your child's future spouse will thank you!

Step 4: **"Fundamentals"** are all basic cleaning. Starting Monday, list 1 to 4 cleaning tasks each day to complete your weekly "Direction of Focus" goals.

Step 5: **"5 O'clock Pick-up."** Doing this fun, energetic activity with your children instills the wonderful habit of keeping their space tidy. Working as a family, set the timer for 15-30 minutes late in the afternoon before dinnertime. Your husband will enjoy the orderly environment after a hard day at work.

Step 6: **"Finale"** space at the bottom is for planning organizational tasks, special cleaning, painting, and maintenance within your "Direction of Focus" for the week.

Cleaning Compass

Week of:			

	Focus 15	Fundamentals	5'O Clock Pick-up
Monday			
Tuesday			
Wednesday			
Thursday			
Friday			

Direction of Focus:

Finale

Meal Planning
Instruction Guide

"Before anything else, preparation is the key to success."
~ Alexander Graham Bell

Feeding the family healthy, delicious meals is a homemaker's privilege and challenge; everyone has to eat! Using the *Meal Planner* will simplify this task by compiling the week's meals, recipe resources, and additional foods to prepare on one page. With planning, your table will be a place to gather family and friends for economical, nutritious, beautiful, delicious food and relaxed, connecting fellowship.

Step 1: **Gather recipes** from various resources such as recipe cards, cook books, magazines, Pinterest, websites, diet programs, etc.

Step 2: In the **"Recipe Resource"** column next to the meal, write the name of the recipe, its resource, and page number.

Step 3: Use the **"Additional Foods"** column to plan out-of-the-ordinary baking, snacks, and appetizers, etc.

Step 4: Check off each box in the **"Prep/Cook/Cleanup"** column as you complete the task.

~ Suggestions ~

- While you have your recipe resources gathered, continue to create meal plans for additional weeks.
- Select quick, healthy recipes that use items frequently in your pantry, fridge, or freezer.
- Before making a hard copy of a new recipe, get the family's approval.
- Transfer digital recipes to hard copies to file them in a designated spot for all family members to use. For a more personal touch, hand-write special recipes for posterity's sake. Think how special it will be for your children and grandchildren to have a favorite recipe written in your hand with notes.
- Store your completed *Meal Planner* forms in a binder, organized by date, and reuse them the same time next year. Create a section in your binder for holiday meal plans to reuse every year.
- Wash, dry, and chop vegetables for specific meals right after grocery shopping. Measure ingredients for specific recipes and store in labeled containers in the refrigerator or freezer.
- Practice the "Focus 15" in the kitchen. Set the timer for yourself to prepare vegetables or unload groceries into the pantry. Make a game for kids to put away leftovers before the timer goes off.

See additional suggestions on page 28.

Meal Planner

Week of: _____	Recipes & Resources	Additional Foods	Prep	Cook	Clean-up
Monday Breakfast Lunch Dinner			☐☐☐	☐☐☐	☐☐☐
Tuesday Breakfast Lunch Dinner			☐☐☐	☐☐☐	☐☐☐
Wednesday Breakfast Lunch Dinner			☐☐☐	☐☐☐	☐☐☐
Thursday Breakfast Lunch Dinner			☐☐☐	☐☐☐	☐☐☐
Friday Breakfast Lunch Dinner			☐☐☐	☐☐☐	☐☐☐
Saturday Breakfast Lunch Dinner			☐☐☐	☐☐☐	☐☐☐
Sunday Breakfast Lunch Dinner			☐☐☐	☐☐☐	☐☐☐

Meal Planning

~ Suggestions ~

- Prepare double recipes and freeze half for the family to re-heat on your busy days, or to share with someone in need.
- Bring your children into the kitchen to learn basic food safety, cooking terms and techniques, measuring, nutrition, etc. Encourage creativity by asking them to modify a recipe or make one up. (Let them make a mess and teach them how to clean up!)
- Experiment with unusual ingredients to expand your children's palates.
- Designate one day weekly, monthly, or quarterly as Intercultural Day and serve only food from a chosen region or country. Have the kids research that culture and share their new knowledge while eating together.
- Use the back side of the *Meal Planner* to write your grocery list.
- Prepare for breakfast the night before. Set the timer on the coffee pot, set the table, etc.

Notes

_____

_____

_____

_____

_____

_____

_____

_____

_____

_____

_____

Weekly Planner
Instruction Guide

> "In their hearts humans plan their course, but the Lord establishes their steps."
> ~ Proverbs 16:9

The **Weekly Planner** is a tool for a busy family to track responsibilities and activities throughout the week. Post it in a central location for everyone to quickly see the week's meal plan, cleaning chores, errands, and family events. Writing down your "to do's" the old-fashioned way, on paper, is very effective. When we write, we remember!

Step 1: **Pray.** Ask the Lord to direct you regarding your commitments on your *Weekly Planner.*

Step 2: **Spend about 15 minutes on Sunday in prayerful consideration**, seeking the Lord as you formulate your intentions for the week.

Step 3: **Write the month and dates** for the week in your planner.

Step 4: **Write your "to-do" list** in the column under the day of the week, and in the row corresponding to the time of day. Include specific times next to the task, if relevant.

Step 5: **Fill in the shaded rows labeled "Breakfast," "Lunch," and "Dinner"** with the menu for those meals each day.

Step 6: **"Notes"** spaces are to jot down ideas, names, directions—whatever comes up.

Step 7: After planning your meals and finding recipes on Sunday using the *Meal Planner* form, **check the boxes in the "Meal Planner" space** at the bottom of the page.

Step 8: As you finish the tasks on your *Cleaning Compass* form each day, **check the boxes in the "Cleaning Compass" space** at the bottom of the page.

Weekly Planner

		Monday	Tuesday	Wednesday
M O R N I N G	**Breakfast:**			
	Notes			
A F T E R N O O N	**Lunch:**			
	Notes			
E V E N I N G	**Dinner:**			
	Notes			

Meal Planner	**Cleaning Compass**	**Cleaning Compass**	**Cleaning Compass**
☐ Recipes & Resources	☐ Focus 15	☐ Focus 15	☐ Focus 15
	☐ Fundamentals	☐ Fundamentals	☐ Fundamentals
☐ Grocery List	☐ 5'o Clock Pick-Up	☐ 5'o Clock Pick-Up	☐ 5'o Clock Pick-Up

Thursday	Friday	Saturday	Sunday

Cleaning Compass
☐ Focus 15
☐ Fundamentals
☐ 5'o Clock Pick-Up

Cleaning Compass
☐ Focus 15
☐ Fundamentals
☐ 5'o Clock Pick-Up

Notes

Notes

Notes

Monthly Planner
Instruction Guide

"Excellence means being YOUR best....being better tomorrow than you were yesterday. Excellence means matching your practice with your potential."
~ Brian Harbour, *Rising above the Crowd*

The **Monthly Planner** is an activity map of all the plans affecting everyone in your home. This tool will keep your family organized and informed. It will show you if you are over-committed, unbalanced, or neglecting priorities. The clarity of seeing how time is spent provides an opportunity to change course, to make choices that align with your values.

Step 1: **Pray.** Ask the Lord to direct you in your commitments before entering them on your *Monthly Planner*.

Step 2: **Write in the month and year.**

Step 3: **Transfer relevant information from** *Weekly Planner* **to** *Monthly Planner*.

Step 4: **Write in appointments,** deadlines, goal progress, practices, games, school events, performances, etc.

Step 5: **"Activities/Traditions" section is to remind you to plan seasonal outings,** family get-togethers, crafts, and new ideas from your *New Additions for New Traditions* form.

~ Suggestions ~

- Print 12 to 18 *Monthly Planners* at once to be ready to write in important events as they become known throughout the year.

- Schedule appointments for less busy months to leave time and energy for holidays and eventful months.

- Pre-book routine doctor visits, haircuts, etc. at the same times each year.

- Make standing beauty appointments for November and December, and keep them to be ready for holiday parties and photos.

- Plan spontaneity if it doesn't come naturally. Block time in your schedule to play.

Monthly Planner

Activities/ Traditions	Monday	Tuesday	Wednesday

Thursday	Friday	Saturday	Sunday

~Gift Giving~
Instruction Guide

"The best gifts are wrapped in love and tied with heartstrings."
~ Zig Ziglar, *Something Else to Smile About*

The **Gift Giving** form centralizes all aspects of this time-honored tradition of generosity. Keep track of gift ideas and purchases for birthdays, anniversaries, graduations, Christmas, etc. for everyone on your list. With this list in your purse, you can make the most of your shopping trips and bargain-hunting. It can also remind you if you already have that gift stashed away in your gift closet, and if it's wrapped and ready to give!

Step 1: **Pray with your husband to ask the Lord to direct you in your gift giving**; how much to budget for gifts, how much to spend on each recipient, specific gift ideas, homemade projects to make, etc. As the Lord lays people on your hearts, thank God for their presence in your life, and reflect on how to bless them through your giving.

Step 2: **Write on your *Gift Giving* form next to "Recipient" the occasion or reason for the gift:** Christmas, birthday, holiday party, welcoming neighbors, graduation, wedding, baby shower, etc.

Step 3: **Use the "Budget" column to record amounts decided upon.**

Step 4: **In the "Gift Item" column, write the gift you have selected.**

Step 5: **Check the "Purchased" column after ordering or buying in the store.**

Step 6: **What a sense of accomplishment to check off the "Wrapped" Column!**

Step 7: **Checking the "Receipt Filed" column** reminds you to store all gift receipts in a large envelope attached to your *Gift Giving* form for easy returns and record-keeping.

Step 8: **Present your labor of love to the recipient with a prayer and a smile.** In showing kindness, YOU have been God's hands and feet!

Step 9: **In the *Gift / Order Complete* column is when items are in hand.** Another defining moment...you've made progress!

~ Suggestions ~

- Divide the shopping with your husband and write his initials next to recipient's name; make a copy for your husband.
- Keep a perpetual gift closet where you store items to give throughout the year, for all occasions. Continuously stock it with discounted items, stocking-stuffers, homemade crafts/art, heirlooms ready to pass on, and gifts you want to re-gift.
    - Ask the Lord, "Who can I bless with these item?"

See additional suggestions on page 38.

Gift Giving

Year:
_____

Recipient	Occasion	Budget	Gift Item	Purchased	Wrapped	Receipt Filed

Gift Giving

"You will be enriched in every way so that you can be generous on every
occasion, and...your generosity will result in thanksgiving to God."
~ 2 Corinthians 9:11

~ Suggestions ~

- When you find the perfect present for someone, attach a note with the recipient's name and occasion to be given before putting it in the gift closet. Enter the information on the *Gift Giving* form for that year.

- When re-gifting, identify the original giver of an item with a note to avoid giving it back to them or to someone they know.

- Refer to previous *Gift Giving* forms so you don't repeat a gift to the same recipient

- Do-it-yourself gifts can be very cost-efficient. You can make the same project for multiple people using supplies and equipment you already have. Start early! Make extras while you are at it.

- Find personalized gifts at craft fairs or through local artisans. For example:
  - Purchase a hand-painted clay pot and fill it with a plant propagated from your own yard.
  - Remake a favorite photo to look like an oil painting.
  - Have a blanket or wall-hanging made from team shirts or baby clothes.

- Consider having the store wrap gifts for a more professional look, or if you are short on time or supplies.

- If shipping gifts:
  - Gather all shipping address information, including recipient phone number, and create mailing labels. Follow the shipper's rules for what can be shipped, and how to label and seal boxes.
  - Keep shipping receipts with confirmation / tracking information in the receipt envelope. Note on the receipt what was shipped.
  - Put a notification in your phone to follow up on package delivery.
  - Avoid holiday shipping hassle and extra cost by mailing well in advance. Third-class rates through the U.S. Post Office are reasonable, but can mean 3-6 weeks before delivery. Military and overseas can take even longer. Better to arrive early than late!

Notes

Gifts Received and Thank You's

"All this is for your benefit, so that the grace that is reaching more and more people may cause thanksgiving to overflow to the glory of God."
~ 2 Corinthians 4:15

The *Gifts Received & Thank You's* form is a reminder to show appreciation for the kindness of those who have graciously blessed you or your family with a gift. Though you probably expressed a verbal "thank you" when given the gift, a hand-written note is a tool to cultivate a grateful heart while making a deeper connection with someone who cares about you. Don't you feel appreciated and loved when someone has taken the time to craft and send a thank you note to you? Model for your children how to receive a gift with enthusiasm and grace, regardless of their personal feelings about the item or the person giving it. Then, coach them to write their own thank you note to bless the giver.

Step 1: **In the "Giver" column, list the names of all those who gifted you or your children.** Make a copy of this form for your children who are old enough to complete the thank you process alone.

Step 2: **Write in the "Gift Received" column details about the gift and card.**

Step 3: **In the "Address" column, write the physical address of the giver.**

Step 4: **The "Special Word" column provides space for notes about how the gift will be used**, a potential benefit of the gift, and how the receiver feels about the gift and about the giver. Make it personal and focus on the giver's intent, sacrifice, thoughtfulness, etc.

Step 5: **Compose a draft by hand, or on the computer if you need spell check.** Read it out loud to yourself, make corrections, and write your final draft on stationary or a note card. Sign your name "Love," "Sincerely," or "With Gratitude," depending on the relationship to the giver. This may become a keepsake, so make it look beautiful!

Step 6: **Check the "Sent" column after the note is written, addressed, stamped, and mailed.**

Gifts Received and Thank You's

Giver	Gift Received	Address	Special Word	Sent

New Additions for New Traditions

"For last year's words belong to last year's language and next year's words await another voice. And to make an end is to make a beginning."
~ T.S. Eliot

Traditions provide connection to the past and, hopefully, anticipation of a special day or season. You can honor those who have gone before by contributing your family's uniqueness to traditions. As you encounter exciting new ideas through travel, reading, and observing others, you may want to incorporate them into your celebration next time. Now, when you experience an activity or discover a yummy recipe, capture the details on the *New Additions for New Traditions* form. Be careful to keep your schedule realistic when adding something; modify, replace, or put on hold practices that don't serve your family right now. The goal is to stay present and create joyful experiences for you and your family.

Step 1: In the "Occasion" column, name the event, season, or holiday to use your new idea.

Step 2: Record the "New Idea" to initiate next year.
Include:
- Events (Christmas Train, fun-run, church Easter Cantata, Nutcracker ballet, etc.)
- Holiday Traditions (practice Lent, make gingerbread house with kids to display in the dining room, etc.)
- Recipes (Easter Carrot Cake, order prepared turkey from grocery store, etc.);
- Children's school, team, and club programs (Spring dance recital, etc.)
- Travel and Vacation ideas

Step 4: The "Action Steps" column is your plan to make your new idea happen. List specific steps for you to do, and when you will do them. Even if the idea won't be implemented for months, start preparing now by shopping, crafting, ordering tickets, training, etc. Make your action steps **S.M.A.R.T.** (**S**pecific, **M**easurable, **A**ctionable, **R**ealistic, **T**ime-bound).

Step 5: Transfer your action steps to your *Weekly Planner*. Add reminders on your phone for steps to take as the day approaches. Schedule the "New Idea" to your *Monthly Planner*.

"It's not how much we have but how much we enjoy, that makes happiness."
~ Charles Spurgeon

New Additions for New Traditions

YEAR:

Occasion	New Idea	Action Steps

Delighted to Decorate

Changing the visual landscape of your home, even slightly, is a refreshing introduction to special times of year, generating a homey warmth, as well as anticipation for the coming celebration. Whether you use your children's hand-turkeys to make placemats, purchase sophisticated linens and arrangements, or assemble your own vignettes with natural objects, this can be a time of fun and creativity for you and your children. Together-time crafting, wrapping presents, and walking through the woods to find pine cones and colorful leaves will turn into great memories that may someday become traditions for your kids.

Holiday decorating can be as elaborate or simple as you decide to make it. For example, some of us for whom Christmas decorating is our favorite thing get energized about making our house look like a winter wonderland, inside and out. There are those who prefer to keep it simple with just a tree so they can focus on traveling, attending events, or cooking. And still others, who have enough on their plate, may choose to enjoy the neighbor's decorations through the picture window. "You do you," in every season of the year and in every season of your life.

Whether you have two boxes of holiday decorations or twenty, this guide will help you break down the decorating process into bite-sized pieces while suggesting organizational tips and ideas for making your celebrations more festive.

Step 1: **Divide the spaces in your house and those extra holiday tasks into "Directions of Focus"** and assign them to specific weeks in the month (as you did for cleaning in the *Cleaning Compass* instructions). By grouping rooms and tasks, you can be more efficient in the decorating process, as well as in how you store your items.

This is an example of "Directions of Focus" for holiday decorating:
- Week 1: Outdoor spaces (entries, porch/deck, house/garage exterior); crafting
- Week 2: Kitchen and dining room; gift wrapping
- Week 3: Indoor living spaces; gift wrapping
- Week 4: Bedrooms and bathrooms; crafting

Step 2: **Budget your time for decorating each "Direction of Focus"** (or focus area) and block out the allotted time on your *Weekly Planner*. Ideally, start planning by September for the Thanksgiving/Christmas/New Year season.

Step 3: **Designate areas for crafting and gift wrapping.** Set up tables. Gather supplies and organize your space, ready to work. If you cannot leave your supplies out, organize them for easy retrieval and storage using a rolling cart or carry-case with divided compartments.

Step 4: **Retrieve storage containers of miscellaneous holiday supplies**, such as: decorative ribbon, burlap/fabric, doilies, linens, random objects, small lights, holiday cooking, entertainment, and decorating resources, etc.

Step 5: **Inspect miscellaneous supplies for dirt or damage**. Place items to be cleaned or repaired in a "fix it" box. Discard unwanted items. Keep these supplies available to use while decorating, crafting, and wrapping for easy access to ideas and extra embellishments.

Step 6: **Retrieve storage container(s) labeled only for that week's "Direction of Focus."** (See below suggestions for storage organization).

Step 7: **Clear a space or set up a table in the focus area.** As you unload container(s), inspect items for dirt and damage. Place items to be cleaned or repaired in the "fix it" box. Discard unwanted items.

Step 8: **Clean and repair items in the "fix it" box.** Distribute to focus area.

Step 9: **Take photos before removing your every-day accessories** for reference when returning them.

Step 10: **Retrieve photos of previous holiday decorations** for reference as you decorate.

Step 11: **Designate empty storage container(s) to pack every-day accessories** for safe keeping as you remove them to make room for holiday decor.

Step 12: **Retrieve stepladder and cleaning supplies.** Clean before decorating, if necessary.

Step 13: **Turn the music on and start decorating! Begin at the highest point in the room, and work your way down to the floor.**

Step 14: **When done for the day, sweep up debris.**

Step 15: **Store container(s) with every-day accessories until after the holidays.**

⌇ Suggestions ⌇

Storage:

- Keep original boxes to store breakable and keepsake ornaments.
- Wrap loose items in tissue paper, bubble wrap, or newspaper to prevent chipping, breaking, and scratching.
- Loosely pack artificial flowers, greenery, garlands, bows, and trees to reduce the need to fluff.
- Stuff bows with tissue paper or plastic grocery bags to keep their shape.
- Label storage containers by season/occasion and "Direction of Focus." We have seasonal storage labels available for print at www.myhelpclubformoms.com. If there is more than one box for each focus area, number each box. ("Fall: Indoor Living Spaces—Hearth/coffee table/small pictures, Box 1 of 1" or "Christmas: Outdoor Spaces—roof lights/hangers, Box 2 of 5").
- Store containers together by season/occasion, then by "Direction of Focus."
- Save time by putting entire vignettes in a large bag inside the container so it can be pulled out together and set in its proper place. (Example: For the fireplace hearth and mantle: candlesticks, rustic frame, garland, flower arrangement, vase, small pictures).
- Store delicate items like candles or old ornaments in a climate controlled space.

Decorating:

- Take pictures of decorations when complete to copy from last year.
- Encourage children to decorate their own rooms and other parts of the house by referring to the photos from previous years.

Organizational Planner ~ Decorating

Delighted to Decorate

- Let your children have a room to decorate any way they want! (Well, almost any way).

  - Use the **C.A.S.E.** Method: **C**opy **A**nd **S**teal **E**verything, to find a new style. Start with one table or curio for now. Make gradual changes each year so you don't get overwhelmed.

- Look through cabinets, closets, and drawers for items you may have forgotten that compliment the theme.

- Use books on side tables for reading, place decorative books on easels to display, or stack themed books to build height as a base to highlight decor.

Crafting and Gift Wrapping:

- Carve pumpkins; paint/glitter natural objects to embellish wrapped packages, make wreaths, or create a display; make Christmas tree ornaments or snowflakes; stringing popcorn.

- Watch videos on wrapping, bow tying, and gift-making at www.helpclubformoms.com.

Notes

_____

_____

_____

_____

_____

_____

_____

_____

_____

_____

_____

Delighted to Decorate

Week of:	Decor	Purchase	Everyday Photo	Holiday Photo

Direction of Focus:

Thanksgiving

Dearest Sister,

Welcome to the week of Thanksgiving! We are so glad you are here. Thankfulness and happiness are contagious. People who demonstrate these two traits are a joy to be around! I yearn to be one of these people, and I'm sure you do too. I want to be a mom, wife, and friend who radiates gratefulness and points those closest to me toward Jesus.

This Thanksgiving, your life is most likely a mixture of pleasure and hardship. Despite what your week may look like, you are called to be thankful in every season. "Give thanks in all circumstances; for this is God's will for you in Christ Jesus" (1 Thessalonians 5:18).

Please remember, mama, that we are so incredibly thankful for you! As a team, we are praying for you this week. Our prayer is for your heart to be filled with contentment, gratitude, and an overwhelming sense of peace. The tone of your home is set by you, and this Thanksgiving has the chance to be a tremendously special one if you start each day with a simple prayer:

> "You are my God, and I will praise you! You are my God, and I will exalt you! Give thanks to the Lord, for he is good! His faithful love endures forever." (Psalm 118:28-29 NLT)

Love,

Rachel Jones and the Help Club For Moms Team

P.S. – Don't forget to print your **free, exclusive printables** available to you at **www.myhelpclubformoms.com**!

> ❝ *It is not how much we have, but how much we enjoy, that makes happiness.* ❞
> ~ *Charles Spurgeon*

Mom Tips

By: Leslie Leonard

The Mom Tips are designed to help you to grow closer to Jesus, offer new ideas to help you to grow in your relationships with your husband and children, and establish a Christ-centered home. At the beginning of each week, simply pray about which tips to try and check them off as you accomplish them. Completing them all or doing only one tip is just fine! As we say in the Help Club, *you do you!!*

The Wise Woman Builds Her Spirit

- Make time to spend at least 15 minutes a day praying and reading your Bible. Take a moment to list five things for which you are thankful. Thank God for all of the ways He shows love to you and your family.
- Be sure to complete each of the three Help Club for Moms Bible studies this week!

The Wise Woman Loves Her Husband

- This Thanksgiving, show love to your husband by loving his family. Pray for them. Be patient, kind, and forgiving, even if your relationship is difficult. Look for the best in them, then be sure to tell them what you love and appreciate about them, in writing or in person. Your Lord and Savior, Jesus, will be well pleased with your kindness. "Blessed are the peacemakers, for they will be called children of God" (Matthew 5:9).
- Pick a night to sit down with your husband after your children have gone to bed. Share what you appreciate and admire about him.

The Wise Woman Loves Her Children

- Make a list of things you are thankful for about each of your children. Set a simple breakfast table (even if you are just eating cereal), light a candle, and read your list out loud to each child on Thanksgiving morning.
- Create a Thanksgiving journal that can be added to each year. Pass it around the table every Thanksgiving to have your guests record their gratitude. This makes beautiful memories for years!

The Wise Woman Cares For Her Home

- Prepare for the busyness of Thanksgiving by cleaning your refrigerator and oven. If you use special plates and serving dishes, wipe them clean.
- Save time and have easy mashed potatoes by cooking them a day or two in advance. Prepare the potatoes, then put them in a casserole dish. When the big day arrives, bake them in the oven to have piping hot potatoes with less time. You can do that with most casseroles, too!

"Above all, love each other deeply,
because love covers over a multitude of sins."

~ 1 Peter 4:8

"Dwelling on your problems doesn't fix them; it just makes you an expert at them."

~ Tommy Newberry

- A big component of the Help Club for Moms is praying with a prayer partner for 10 minutes once a week. If you don't have a prayer partner, pray and ask God to bring her to you! He is faithful and will provide!
- It's time to meet with Jesus! Oh, how He loves you and me! Pray today for Jesus to speak to your heart, and help you and your family feel His love—the wide and long and high and deep love of Jesus (Ephesians 3:18). Ask Him to help you love others the way He loves you.
- Read 1 Peter 4:8. Ask Jesus to speak to you about loving your family and friends deeply.

Where Do You Shine Your Spotlight?

By: Deb Weakly

Thanksgiving week is here and our hearts are drawn to all the nostalgia of home and family. We long for the delicious smells of turkey, au-gratin potatoes, and pumpkin pies cooking in the oven, and the sounds of people laughing and having fun together while the kids run all around the house.

As moms of the home, we have worked so hard to get to this day. The shopping, cooking, and decorating have all been completed. Now all we need is for the family to arrive so the festivities can begin. And, for some families, this is where the hard part of our holiday season can often begin—when the family arrives.

I meet sweet moms all over the place who have been hurt by the ones closest to them. The holidays serve as reminders of a harsh word spoken or a wound unhealed. These memories can steal the joy of precious time spent with family.

Some have family members who get on their nerves after time spent together, and cause irritation as each day passes until everyone goes home. As I speak with these sweet moms I say one phrase to them that I feel can help make their holidays better, and I thought I would share this with you too:

Where do you shine your spotlight? In other words, what do you choose to focus on in the other person?

In our minds, we all have a "spotlight" with which we shine on the good or the not-so-good aspects of people and circumstances simply by what we think about. Our thoughts and attention go to where we focus—for better or for worse. So when you think about a particular loved one, do you think about the hurt, wound, or annoying habits, or do you see a fellow human being in need of a Savior and unconditional love as we do?

I would love to share a few Scriptures and tips to help your holiday season be the best it can possibly be. As with everything else in life, I believe the Lord wants us mamas to come to Him with our bitterness, burdens, and sadness. He wants us to focus on His goodness and His everlasting, healing Word, and choose to love like Jesus as much as possible.

When we go to God's Word, we read things like:

- Be content (Hebrews 13:5, Philippians 4:11)
- Get rid of all bitterness (Ephesians 4:31)
- Love one another deeply (1 Peter 4:8)
- Be thankful (1 Thessalonians 5:18)
- Count your blessings (Psalm 118:1, Ephesians 5:20, 1 Thessalonians 5:16-18)
- Forgive (Colossians 3:13, Ephesians 4:32)
- Stay hopeful and believe the best intentions of others (1 Corinthians 13:7) (Philippians 4:8)

May I suggest writing these verses down in your journal or in dry erase marker on your bathroom mirror to keep them close to you during the holiday season?

Sweet friend, it all boils down to keeping our eyes fixed on Jesus, meditating on the Scriptures, praying, and obeying by faith, especially in the area of relationships. Do what Philippians 4:8 says and think true, excellent, honorable, and lovely thoughts. Refuse to think bitter, resentful, critical, or unkind thoughts.

Ask God to help you think like Jesus, love like Jesus, and forgive like Jesus. Assume the best as much as possible. Pray to see people the way God does, and ask Him to help you to love them as He does. Spotlight the good!

Where's your spotlight focused? When you look at others what do you see?

Questions to Ponder:

- Ask God to give you three positive qualities about each person you will see this Thanksgiving.
- Ask God to fill you with His love for each and every one of them.
- Pray for them to come to know Jesus if they haven't already, and pray for God to bring them joy this holiday season.
- Ask God to show you how to be a blessing to them this week. Write it down in your journal, and keep praying this week for a wonderful Thanksgiving holiday!

Faith-Filled Ideas:

Buy a small bunch of flowers for your table if you are hosting the meal. Get small vases and arrange the flowers to make the table more inviting. If you are going to someone's home for dinner, bring a lovely inexpensive bouquet of flowers as a thank-you gift for the hostess.

Purchase a thank-you note and write a lovely note to the host and hostess of your Thanksgiving meal.

Be a blessing this Thanksgiving! Offer to help clean up and then do it! Stay in the kitchen until the last plate is clean.

Make sure to say "thank you" many times for the meal, and again as you are leaving. Highlight your favorite part of the meal. Be generous with your kind words!

journal

journal

_____
_____
_____
_____
_____
_____
_____
_____
_____
_____
_____
_____
_____
_____
_____
_____
_____
_____
_____
_____
_____
_____
_____
_____
_____
_____
_____

"Rejoice in the Lord always. I will say it again: Rejoice!
Let your gentleness be evident to all. The Lord is near.
Do not be anxious about anything, but in every situation,
by prayer and petition, with thanksgiving,
present your requests to God."

~ Philippians 4:4-6

"Prayer is God's ordained way to bring His miracle power to bear in human need."
~ Wesley L. Duewel

- Dear Sister, it's time to gather your Bible and journal, and spend time with Jesus. Is it cold where you live this time of year? Grab your favorite sweater or blanket and snuggle in for our devotional reading today.

- Take time to read these accounts: Matthew 14:19-20, Matthew 15:36-37, and Mark 8:1-9.

Miracles of Multiplication

By: Rae-Ellen Sanders

I have always been awed by the miracle story of the five loaves and two fish! In this incredible miracle of multiplication, Jesus first took time to give thanks for the little He had. Our Heavenly Father then multiplied the loaves and fish so generously that there was not only enough to feed thousands, but there were 12 baskets full of leftovers! Authentic thanksgiving is a key step to receiving blessings.

We reserve the fourth Thursday in November to celebrate traditions, with lots of eating, and hopefully, lots of gratitude given unto the Lord! Consequently, this time of year can also highlight the areas in our lives that we experience lack or discontentment. Perhaps it's your finances—that's usually what we think of first. How about the size of your home, your wardrobe, etc? We can all find something we wished we had more of! Instead of focusing on what you want, or even need, thank God for the blessings you already have. When we offer a sacrifice of praise, even during hard times, we take the attention off of ourselves and place it on the Almighty God. Thanksgiving conquers our discontentment, and we gain the discipline of rejoicing always!

My mama used to say, "There will always be people who have more than you and those who will have less than you." Don't get caught up in the comparison game! This tactic of the enemy makes you miserable! The enemy likes to camp in this area of your heart; but when you count your blessings and are thankful for what you have, Satan packs up and moves out!

Questions to Ponder:

- How has God blessed you? Write these blessings in your journal. Write down even the smallest thing for which you are grateful. Challenge yourself to see how long you can make your list. Pray and record the attributes and spiritual gifts you have been given, thank God for them, and ask Him to mature you in these areas. If you have a material need, first thank God for the little you have and then praise Him for being your Provider, your Jehovah-jirah.

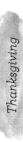

Faith-Filled Ideas:

Mama, if we want blessings and miracles in our lives, we must be thankful at all times, and not just on Thanksgiving Day! Make a habit of being thankful every day—starting this week!

Journal

_____

_____

_____

_____

_____

_____

_____

_____

_____

_____

_____

_____

_____

_____

_____

_____

_____

_____

_____

_____

_____

_____

_____

> "It is good to praise the Lord and make music
> to your name, O Most High, proclaiming your love
> in the morning and your faithfulness at night."
>
> ~ Psalm 92:1-2

"The best and most beautiful things in the world cannot be seen or even touched.
They must be felt with the heart."
~ Helen Keller

- It's time to meet with your precious Savior! He is the Light of the World, the Lamb of God who loves you more than you could ever comprehend!

- Read Psalm 92:1-15. Write verses one and two in your journal. Give thanks to God for His unfailing love and faithfulness to you and your family. Ask Him to help you focus on Christ this Christmas and not on what the world says is important. Pray for the Holy Spirit to fill you with love and kindness.

Happy Holy Days

By: Mary Frieg

With the Lord's help, we can keep the holy days that are upon us from being just holidays.

The word "holiday" originally meant "holy day." Sadly, the term "holidays" now simply means the period from November to New Year's. It has become a materialistic call to celebrate that has blurred the true meaning of the holidays. While there is nothing wrong with making our homes festive and cheerful, we must be careful not to exhaust our time, resources, and energy on less important things.

Proverbs 17:1 says, "Better a dry crust with peace and quiet than a house full of feasting with strife." Last Christmas, my wonderful brother visited my family during an unusually busy season. In the month of December alone, my husband and I traveled out of town, our youngest son got married, and we hosted many family and friends in our home. Needless to say, there was much stress and busyness!

There was one particular incident that stands out in my mind that I would like to share with you. My brother was helping me around the house and asked me where to put various items in an effort to help me tidy up. (I have a great brother!) I was feeling unusually burdened with my workload and I snapped at my dear, sweet brother. I felt terrible! I realized later that I had allowed myself to become overwhelmed with tasks I wanted to accomplish, rather than loving my family.

Have you ever been inside a perfectly decorated home that was lovely to look at but the fruit of the Spirit was not in it? Showing love and being like Jesus to our loved ones is much more important than having "House Beautiful!" Your family cares more about having a happy mom than they do about having a perfect house. This Christmas, while the magazines and catalogs call upon us to do everything perfectly, may we decide in our hearts to do fewer and simpler things, with love and kindness.

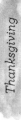

As Jesus said to Martha, "You are worried about so many things, but Mary has chosen the better part." May we all choose the better part by resting in the love of Jesus this Holy-day season!

Questions to Ponder:

- What do I need to give up to the Lord to be fully present for my family during the holidays? In what areas am I tempted to overdo and shortchange my family's spiritual benefit?

- What spiritual components can I provide to my holiday celebrations to make them truly Holy days that draw my children to the Lord?

Faith-Filled Ideas:

Keep Thanksgiving from being squeezed out. Put up Christmas decorations after Thanksgiving to keep its message a separate priority.

This Thanksgiving, let everyone around your table have an opportunity to express something they are thankful for before or after saying grace. This will help them be participants rather than spectators. Some families do this by dropping a kernel of corn into a basket and mentioning something they are thankful for.

When Thanksgiving is over, let the first Christmas decoration you bring out be the nativity scene, emphasizing Jesus' birth as the reason for the Christmas season.

journal

_____
_____
_____
_____
_____
_____
_____
_____
_____
_____
_____
_____
_____
_____

I just love that every September the world at large suggests drinking pumpkin creamer in their coffee. It's as if fall doesn't start until I have my hands wrapped around this warm beverage. As anyone with a coffee addiction knows, specialty coffees can really add up and make a dent in your budget. This homemade version is super yummy in comparison, cost-effective, and can be tweaked to your liking! Oh, and the extra benefit is that your home will smell delicious, so no need for pumpkin spice candles. Did I mention that you make it in your crockpot? Just dump in the ingredients and let those spices get acquainted!

CROCKPOT PUMPKIN SPICE LATTE

By: Rae-Ellen Sanders

Ingredients

6 cups whole milk
(vanilla almond milk is an amazing substitution)

6 cups strong brewed coffee, cooled

½ cup pumpkin puree

4 Tbsp vanilla extract

½ cup brown sugar

2 tsp pumpkin pie spice

½ tsp cinnamon

2-3 cinnamon sticks

Directions:

1. Add brewed coffee and milk of choice in your crockpot.

2. In separate bowl, mix pumpkin puree, brown sugar, vanilla extract, and spices.

3. Combine mixture in crock pot and stir.

4. Toss in cinnamon sticks and cover.

5. Cook on high for 2 hours.

6. This will obviously render quite a bit of coffee to consume. Invite friends over for an afternoon of fellowship or store leftovers in the fridge. Reheat in the microwave or try your Pumpkin Latte over ice.

10 Scriptures to Pray this Thanksgiving

1. **Psalm 118:1** – "Give thanks to the Lord, for he is good; his love endures forever."

2. **Psalm 118:24** – "The Lord has done it this very day; let us rejoice today and be glad."

3. **Ephesians 5:20** – "Always giving thanks to God the Father for everything, in the name of our Lord Jesus Christ."

4. **Psalm 95:2** – "Let us come before him with thanksgiving and extol him with music and song."

5. **1 Thessalonians 5:16-18** – "Rejoice always, pray continually, give thanks in all circumstances; for this is God's will for you in Christ Jesus."

6. **Philippians 4:6** – "Do not be anxious about anything, but in every situation, by prayer and petition, with thanksgiving, present your requests to God."

7. **Colossians 4:2** – "Devote yourselves to prayer, being watchful and thankful."

8. **2 Corinthians 4:15** – "All this is for your benefit, so that the grace that is reaching more and more people may cause thanksgiving to overflow to the glory of God."

9. **2 Corinthians 9:11** – "You will be enriched in every way so that you can be generous on every occasion, and through us your generosity will result in thanksgiving to God."

10. **Colossians 3:17** – "And whatever you do, whether in word or deed, do it all in the name of the Lord Jesus, giving thanks to God the Father through him."

Thankfulness
Photo Scavenger Hunt

By: Tara Davis

Do you need a fun activity your kids can do while you make Thanksgiving dinner or spend time visiting with family? Have a Photo Scavenger Hunt!

1. Grab a camera of some sort for each child or split up into teams and let the Thanksgiving fun begin!

2. Give each team or child a copy of this photo scavenger hunt list.

3. Ask them to check items off as they photograph things they are thankful for.

4. Set a time limit if you would like, and encourage them to really think about it and get creative!

5. Have them share their pictures with the family afterwards and talk about all of the ways we can thank God each and every day of the year.

Take a picture of something you are thankful for....

- [ ] That is in nature
- [ ] That smells amazing
- [ ] That is bright and cheerful
- [ ] That you can snuggle
- [ ] That you like to read
- [ ] That is a person you care about
- [ ] That tastes delicious
- [ ] That has been hard for you
- [ ] That makes you laugh
- [ ] That makes a beautiful sound
- [ ] That makes you feel safe
- [ ] That is your favorite color
- [ ] That is special to you
- [ ] That is a place you love
- [ ] That you would like to share with others
- [ ] That is older than you
- [ ] That is fun to do with others
- [ ] That you have learned

∼ Bonus ∼
∼ Craft Idea ∼

Make a Thanksgiving Table Runner Keepsake!

Materials:

- A solid, light-colored table runner
- Bright-colored acrylic craft paint (found at Walmart or a craft store)
- Thick paintbrushes
- A permanent marker
- Have baby wipes or a washcloth on hand for easy cleanup

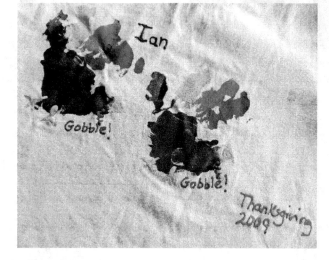

Directions:

1. Paint each child's hand and quickly press it evenly onto the table runner.

2. Add the child's name and year under each handprint with a permanent marker.

3. You can even use a permanent marker to embellish the handprint to look like a turkey, adding eye, beak, gobbler, and legs.

4. Each Thanksgiving season, adding handprints will turn into a fun tradition while keeping a record of your children's growth.

Christmas Handprint Tree Skirt Craft Idea!

Make a handprint tree skirt this Christmas! Simply take a plain felt tree scarf and make handprints by painting your child's hands with acrylic paint and pressing them into the tree skirt, using the same materials listed above. Write the child's name and year. Repeat each year and watch your children grow!

Christmas

~ Week One ~

Hello Mom,

Welcome to week one of the most wonderful time of the year!

The Christmas season can be a little chaotic here at my house. With decorating, shopping, and a half-dozen Pinterest projects vying for my attention, I often find myself off course. I do so much, yet so little of it actually matters in the lives of my children.

This year, my desire is to be more intentional about communicating Christ's love to my family. Will you join me in seeking to reflect the heart of Jesus to your children, as you light up their world with love this Christmas?

Here's the plan, my friends:

- Teach (and re-teach) the story of Jesus! There are several beautiful Advent or Jesse Tree books you can use to make this easy. We are using *Unwrapping the Greatest Gift* by Ann Voskamp this year, and we enjoy *Truth in the Tinsel* for the preschool years.

- Spend time playing with your children. Instead of searching Amazon for the greatest new toy, spend time together playing with their old favorite toys and games. Your time and attention is the best gift you can give this Christmas.

- Make fun traditions together! Your children will likely forget the new Christmas recipe you try this year, the perfectly wrapped presents, and the Pinterest-worthy decorations. However, your yearly traditions, regardless of simplicity or silliness, will become some of the building blocks of their childhood memories.

- Speak LIFE over them. We need to make words of love the carol we sing daily this Christmas! It is easy for me to get snippy when I am busy, but it is my words that will form how my boys view themselves (and their Savior too). Will you join me in my goal for this December: *to make a habit of speaking love, every word, every day*?

- Smile! My children's happiness this season will be impacted more by the joy I demonstrate than by any other fun holiday experience I provide. I want my face and my actions to shine the light of my Savior's love!

With love,

Tara Davis and the Help Club For Moms Team

> "*All the Christmas presents in the world are worth nothing without the presence of Christ.*"
>
> *~ Dr. David Jeremiah*

By: Leslie Leonard

> "For to us a child is born, to us a son is given, and the government will be on his shoulders. And he will be called Wonderful Counselor, Mighty God, Everlasting Father, Prince of Peace." ~ Isaiah 9:6

The Wise Woman Builds Her Spirit

- Make time in your schedule for regular Bible study and prayer this Christmas season. Holiday busyness can be overwhelming, so time with God is more essential than ever to keep your sense of inner peace.
- Record Philippians 4:4-7, Proverbs 16:3, and Ephesians 4:2 using a voice recording app on your phone. Listen to them daily to help you stay focused and at peace with your family.

The Wise Woman Loves Her Husband

- Stay connected to your husband with a scheduled date night. Get extra rest and plan time alone for fun and intimacy. Feeling connected is the best gift you can give to one another and to your family.
- Plan a time to sit down with your husband to prayerfully create a budget for Christmas. Make a commitment to each other to work as a team to stay within your budget. Pray together to ask God for help.

The Wise Woman Loves Her Children

- Involve your children in planning an activity that will help them share the love of Jesus with their community. Who can you help as a family this Christmas season? Be excited with them and enthusiastically support their willingness, generosity, and creativity.
- This December, play Christmas music in your home most days. Be sure to have fun singing and dancing with your kids.

The Wise Woman Cares For Her Home

- How's your Christmas organization going? Have you finished planning using the Best Holiday Season Ever organizational planner? If not, be sure to carve out a little time this week to plan your Christmas season using the instructions and forms provided.
- Set up a gift wrapping station with tape, scissors, yardstick, boxes of various sizes, wrapping paper, gift bags, tissue paper, ribbon/bows/decorations, and gift tags. To save stress, wrap gifts as you buy them, and put them under the tree to create anticipation for the kids.

"A voice of one calling:
'In the wilderness prepare the way for the Lord;
make straight in the desert a highway for our God.'"

~ Isaiah 40:3

"The only people whose soul can truly magnify the Lord are...people who acknowledge their lowly estate and are overwhelmed by the coming of the magnificent God."
~ John Piper

- Call your prayer partner for your 10-minute prayer call. Keep trying to connect until you can pray together. This little habit of praying regularly with a friend will truly change your life!

- This is the day that the Lord has made! Wake up, grab your Bible, journal, and a pen, and get ready to spend some precious moments with your Savior.

- Read Isaiah 40:1-5. Write verse three in your journal and ask yourself if you have prepared a place for the Lord in your heart.

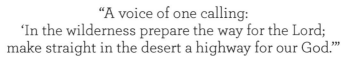

Celebrating Advent During a Busy Christmas Season

By: Rachel Jones

Advent is a season of preparation and waiting for the celebration of Jesus' birth at Christmas. The term advent is from the Latin translation of "coming." God's prophecies in the Old Testament prepared the way for His promise. He told us He was coming and then He fulfilled that promise!

Honoring Advent teaches our children the real reason for Christmas, creates memories with our children they will cherish forever, and allows our families to spend quality time together, focusing on what is good, pure, and holy. We will experience a more peaceful holiday season when we keep Jesus at the center.

Luke 2:13-14 tells us that, "Suddenly a great company of the heavenly host appeared with the angel, praising God and saying, Glory to God in the highest, and on earth peace to those on whom His favor rests."

This verse is so commanding and powerful! Mamas, let us all commit to teaching our children in a tangible way just how much that verse changes their lives forever!

- **Celebrating with a Jesse Tree:**
  Jesse trees are a very old Christmas tradition that first started in Medieval Times. They are used to help tell the story of the Bible from creation to the Christmas Story. The name comes from Jesse who was the Father of the great Jewish King David. Isaiah 11:1-4 tells the prophecy of Jesse.

- **Using an Advent Calendar to Count Down the Days to Christmas:**
  Younger children especially enjoy using something tangible to count down to Christmas. Our family favorite is a traditional Advent calendar with little, individual boxes. Every day, my girls pull out a small piece of paper with something for us to read together–either a short verse or a page from our Jesus Storybook Bible. I also put a second piece of paper with a craft idea, activity, or special snack to share. Some ideas include making cookies for a neighbor, wrapping our family's presents side-by-side, and dancing to Christmas music together. The possibilities are endless. This planned fun ensures that my family is enjoying one another every day during the month of December.

- **Incorporating a Christian alternative to "Elf on the Shelf":**
  I like to call it "Mary and Joseph traveling to Bethlehem." Each day, the journey to Jesus' birth draws nearer. Your children will love waking up every morning to find the Mary and Joseph figurines from your nativity set in a different spot.

- **Reading Christmas Books:**
  December is the perfect time to gather the family to enjoy a well-loved Christmas book. My girls get so excited to snuggle under a fleece throw blanket on the couch, or sit together in the kitchen sipping hot chocolate for storytime. (Hot cocoa spilled on the couch really ruins the mood, so better safe than sorry!)

  This list has some of our favorites:
  - *Alabaster's Song: Christmas through the Eyes of an Angel* by Max Lucado
  - *What Is Christmas?* by Michelle Medlock Adams
  - *Stable Where Jesus Was Born* by Rhonda Gowler Greene
  - *There Was No Snow on Christmas Eve* by Pamela Munoz Ryan
  - *The Legend of the Candy Cane* by Lori Walburg
  - *The Small One* by Alex Walsh
  - *The Perfect Christmas Gift (Gigi, God's Little Princess)* by Sheila Walsh
  - *The Candle in the Window* by Grace Johnson

Go to www.helpclubformoms.com/christmas-day-one to read more about all of these special ideas!

Questions to Ponder:

- Which one of these Advent ideas will work for your family? Spend some time in prayer and ask the Lord to guide you in planning this season. Ask for peace and patience as you are preparing and ask for the Lord to open your children's hearts to the joy and wonder of their Savior this Christmas.

Faith-Filled Ideas:

Choose one (or more) of these Advent ideas to become a tradition for your family. Start slowly and be easy on yourself if you begin late or miss a day. Remember the most important thing is that you and your husband are being intentional with your children in pointing them toward Christ.

journal

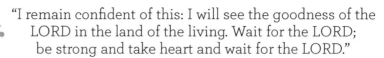

"I remain confident of this: I will see the goodness of the
LORD in the land of the living. Wait for the LORD;
be strong and take heart and wait for the LORD."

~ Psalm 27:13-14

*"However many blessings we expect from God, His infinite liberality will
always exceed all our wishes and our thoughts."*
~ John Calvin

- Oh, how your Savior loves you! Come and meet with Him with expectation today. You are favored! Take out your Bible and notebook. Play some beautiful instrumental music during your time with the Lord today.

- Read Psalm 27:1-14 and 1 Thessalonians 4:16-17. Highlight or write Psalm 27:13-14 in your journal.

Expecting God

By: Tara Fox

Is there anything cuter than a toddler in footie jammies? I just love it!

As I was thinking about expecting God, this is the picture He laid on my heart: Three sweet little ones all zipped up in their jammies, staring with wonderful excitement at their Christmas tree!

Do you remember this feeling of pure joy and anticipation? Did you know this is the way our benevolent Father in Heaven wants us to look to Him–in expectation of His presence and His work in our lives with delight and contemplation?

The word Advent means "coming." For Christians, Advent is a time to look forward to Christ's final return and the fulfillment of his plan—His second coming. We are longingly waiting for our King!

This Advent season, He wants us to wait in expectation for the good things He has for us before His return:

- To gaze upon His face with excitement.
- To revel in His amazing love for us and to wait for the dreams He has laid on our hearts.
- To expect is to know that something will certainly happen!

"For the LORD God is a sun and shield; the LORD bestows favor and honor; no good thing does he withhold from those whose walk is blameless" (Psalm 84:11). We can expect favor, honor, and good things from God!

"Then Jesus said, 'Did I not tell you that if you believe, you will see the glory of God?'" (John 11:40).

Oh, what will He do in our lives if we are daughters who believe? Let us be daughters of the Mighty King who believe we will see the glory of God, and who walk in faith knowing and expecting God to bring His good works to fruition.

As sure as He is coming again, we can expect His goodness and blessings to manifest in our lives! Take this season to look to your Heavenly Father as a child looks forward to Christmas. Just between you and God, when you see a Christmas tree, decoration, or nativity scene this season, smile and let it be a reminder of not only His goodness now, but also of His future return to claim you—His precious daughter for eternity!

Questions to Ponder

- Are you in a season where you have lost your zeal for the Lord? Pray and ask Him to return it to you. Set aside time to spend with God. Our faith is not based on feelings, but instead, our faith is based on a person, Jesus Christ. When we continue to spend time with Him, we are moving in the direction of faith instead of doubt, which leads to anticipation!

- Write and display a running list of the many good things God has done for you over the years. Have a family worship night to thank Him!

Faith-Filled Ideas

Ask the Lord for a Christmas devotion to do with your family. *Christmas Carols for a Kids Heart* has been one of our favorites! Your family will learn the true stories behind the songwriters of favorite Christmas hymns. It is simple, beautifully illustrated, and comes with a CD. It is a great way to start or end your day in the season of Advent!

journal

journal

_____
_____
_____
_____
_____
_____
_____
_____
_____
_____
_____
_____
_____
_____
_____
_____
_____
_____
_____
_____
_____
_____
_____
_____

"Be very careful, then, how you live—not as unwise
but as wise, making the most of every opportunity,
because the days are evil."

~ Ephesians 5:15-16

"He is no fool who gives what he cannot keep to gain that which he cannot lose."
~ Jim Elliot

- It's time to meet with Jesus, the One who gave all He had so you can live a life everlasting with Him! Ask the Holy Spirit to speak to your heart and teach you how to pass your faith on to your children this Christmas.

- Read Ephesians 5:15-16 and Revelation 6:9. Write both of these Scriptures in your journal.

Passing Down the Stories

By: Deb Weakly

In light of the many events around the world in which faithful lovers of Jesus Christ are martyred, my heart cries out for help and understanding. I wish I knew their names and their stories: the martyrs of past and present, whose biographies of life and death, though exceedingly numerous, have great power with which to teach us to live victoriously. I know one day in Heaven we will celebrate each of these precious saints, and behold the whole narrative of their beautiful faith in Jesus Christ.

The lyrics from the well-loved Christmas hymn, "Peace on earth, and goodwill towards men," reflect some of the gentle aspects of Jesus. But as we remember the Christ Child, may we remember that although Jesus came to bring peace to earth, the Scriptures clearly state that He also came to bring a sword to our world, and even to His own mother's soul:

> Then Simeon blessed them and said to Mary, his mother: This child is destined to cause the falling and rising of many in Israel, and to be a sign that will be spoken against so that the thoughts of many hearts will be revealed. And a sword will pierce your own soul too. (Luke 2:34-35)

Jesus Himself told His disciples of the oncoming persecution and how simply believing in Him will force them to give their own lives as a sacrifice for their faith: "Do not suppose that I have come to bring peace to the earth. I did not come to bring peace, but a sword" (Matthew 10:34).

This prophecy of Jesus came true, and millions of courageous Christians have given their lives for their faith down through the ages since the death of Jesus. It is impossible to know each of their stories, but thankfully, I do know some. We tried to pass some of these stories down to our children, and one of my favorites is the story of St. Lucia.

Since she is remembered at Christmastime, on December 13, I would love to share her story with you:

St. Lucia lived in Italy in the fourth century and resolved to live her life devoted to Christ and not to marry. Nevertheless, her mother arranged for her marriage to a Roman soldier, but Lucia refused.

Her heart was so committed to Jesus that she sold her dowry upon hearing about the Christians starving while hiding in the catacombs to flee persecution. She took the money from her dowry and brought food down to the Christians in their hiding places. Since it was dark, she made a crown of torches to light her way.

When her fiancée learned of her betrayal, he turned her over to the Roman authorities. She was tried and found guilty. The customary sentence for a woman without a dowry was life in a brothel. They couldn't move her, however, so they brought materials for a fire and stacked them around her. When the fire would not light, a soldier ended her brave life with a spear.

I can only imagine her excitement waking up to Jesus holding her face in His hands saying, "Well done, good and faithful servant."

St. Lucia lived a beautiful depiction of Christian dedication and sacrifice worth honoring. That is why we remember to pass down her brave story in celebration of her life.

Take every opportunity to teach your children about Christ and the ones who have gone before who have lived and died by faith. Make your family traditions meaningful and fun, with Christ at the center as much as possible.

May we all pass on their courageous stories to the next generation.

Questions to Ponder:

- Who is your favorite faithful Christian or martyr and why?

- How can you best emulate their life in your world?

Faith-Filled Ideas:

As parents, we should use every opportunity to teach our children about the faithful saints who went before us and gave their lives for Christ.

For many years, our family has passed down the faithful story of St. Lucia. On the morning of December 13, I wake up my family wearing a crown of candles and carrying a tray of tea and gingerbread cookies called Pepparkakor. Imagine the excitement for a young child munching on a cookie while in bed, and hear the stories of St. Lucia and her often forgotten peers.

Below is a delicious recipe by the wonderful Phyllis Stanley for delicious Pepparkakor cookies!

St. Lucia day is now a national holiday in Sweden. It is delightful to watch each year's celebration on the internet. I am thankful they remember her brave life.

journal

_____

_____

_____

_____

_____

Food for the Soul

St. Lucia Day is a Swedish holiday on December 13th. Because of the long, cold, dark winters, Swedes welcome this holiday of light. Legend tells us of a lovely, Christian girl from Sicily who risked her life in order to feed the persecuted Christians who were hiding in the catacombs. Because her tray was so filled with provisions, she needed to put candles in a wreath on her head to light the way. We remember this holiday by dressing up in a long white nightgown, with an artificial crown of lights on our heads and pepparkakor for each child.

PEPPARKAKOR (GINGER COOKIES)

By: Phyllis Stanley

Ingredients

1 cup softened butter

2 Tbsp dark corn syrup

1 egg

2-4 Tbsp heavy cream

3 ¼ cups flour

1 ½ cups brown sugar

2 tsp baking soda

3 tsp each of ginger, cinnamon & cloves

Directions:

1. Preheat oven to 350 degrees.

2. With a dough hook, mix together the ingredients.

3. Refrigerate overnight.

4. Roll and cut into heart shapes. Place on greased cookie sheets or cover cookie sheets with parchment paper.

5. Bake at 350 degrees for 10-15 minutes. Cool and then decorate.

Christmas Kindness Challenge

By: Tara Davis

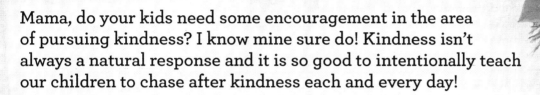

Mama, do your kids need some encouragement in the area of pursuing kindness? I know mine sure do! Kindness isn't always a natural response and it is so good to intentionally teach our children to chase after kindness each and every day!

Christmas happens to be a fabulous time to remind our kids of the kindness Jesus has shown to us! So snuggle up together and read about this wonderful Christmas Kindness Challenge that your kids can enjoy the whole month of December! Just follow the steps below!

Directions:

1. Make copies of the stained glass page for each child, found on page 77, or print copies off our website at **www.myhelpclubformoms.com**.
   Tip: For the activity to work, there can be no words printed on the back of the stained glass coloring sheet and it must be colored in boldly with markers.

2. Read the following paragraphs aloud:

   The Christmas season is the perfect time to develop the habit of sharing Christ's love with others! Through small acts of kindness shown to others, you are actually illuminating the love of Christ in such a beautiful way! Have you ever seen a stained glass window in a church or an old building? It appears to be just a picture made of glass until the radiant sun shines behind it. As the light of the sun shines through the stained glass window, it is truly a magnificent sight!

   It is the same with our acts of kindness. Anyone can do kind things for people, but if the light of the Son (Jesus) is in us, then those acts become glorious shining examples of Christ's love! Do you have Jesus living in you? Are you following Him? If so, do these kind things out of love for Jesus and pour out His love to others at Christmas this year! If you do not follow Jesus and would like to, then it is as easy as the "ABC's"—

   A*dmit to God you're a sinner (Romans 3:23),*
   B*elieve that Jesus is God's Son (John 3:16), and*
   C*onfess your faith in Jesus as your Lord and Savior (Romans 10:9).*

Activity Instructions:

1. On the next page is a list of kind things you can do to spread the love of Jesus. Add your own ideas to this list and then get to work!

2. As you accomplish an act of kindness, color a section of the stained glass coloring page.

3. As the picture is slowly filled in, put the coloring page up to the window and see the light shining through all of your kind deeds.

4. Look for ways to show Christ's love to others. More importantly, make sure the light of Jesus is in you! He is what makes everything truly beautiful!

Christmas Kindness
Challenge

Acts of Kindness for Kids:

- [ ] Go through your toys and donate ones you don't play with to charity or a local children's hospital.
- [ ] Help a sibling or a friend do a chore or other job.
- [ ] Write grandparents a letter or draw a picture and mail it to them.
- [ ] Leave a little treat in the mailbox for the mailman.
- [ ] Donate books you no longer read or need.
- [ ] Put money in the Salvation Army bucket.
- [ ] Make breakfast for your mom or dad.
- [ ] Take a treat to the local fire station.
- [ ] Give a hug to someone who is hurting.
- [ ] Go to a nursing home to visit residents or make and send cards to them.
- [ ] Forgive your sibling or friend when he or she hurts your feelings.
- [ ] Hold the door for people behind you.
- [ ] Write a kind sidewalk message with chalk or in the snow.
- [ ] Make a treat and a Christmas card for the school bus driver or crossing guard.
- [ ] Offer to take the neighbor's dog for a walk.
- [ ] Write a letter to a military member.
- [ ] Share something that is extra-special to you with a sibling or friend.
- [ ] Smile at every single person you see for one whole day.
- [ ] Write a thank-you note to your parents or teacher.
- [ ] Pray for someone.
- [ ] Make a homemade gift for someone.
- [ ] Go buy inexpensive socks, beanies, and mittens (the dollar store has lots of great ones!) and deliver them to a homeless shelter or keep them in your car and hand them out if you come across anyone in need.
- [ ] Make someone laugh.
- [ ] Do something special for a friend.
- [ ] Call a relative who may need cheering up.
- [ ] Invite someone who lives alone over for dinner.
- [ ] For one day, try to pick up at least three pieces of trash wherever you are.
- [ ] Sit with someone at lunch who looks lonely or who doesn't have very many friends.
- [ ] Compliment at least five people in one day.
- [ ] Do something your parents need you to do without being asked.
- [ ] Make a homemade bird feeder and hang it outside (like a pinecone rolled in peanut butter and birdseed).
- [ ] Take cookies to your neighbor.
- [ ] Clean up a mess you didn't make.
- [ ] Draw a picture for mom and dad.
- [ ] Tell someone about Jesus.

Stained Glass Coloring Activity

Advent House

By: Tara Davis

Merry Christmas sweet friends! Are you looking for a Christ-centered Advent activity to do with your children? Look no further! This Advent Christmas House will add a dose of truth and beauty to your children's lives each day of Advent!

You can make this as simple or involved as you would like, just seek the Lord for what He wants you to do this Christmas season! Each day of Advent will feature a Scripture passage for you to read as well as a little picture for your child to color in their house (see pages 84–85). However, we know you are busy moms so there are two open days each week with just a blank window or door for your child to color. Take these days whenever you need them! There is also an optional activity to take the daily Scripture a little bit further, but feel free to do as much or as little as you would like! Now on to the fun preparation!

Prepare: We recommend doing the following things to prepare for this fun activity. Again, make this activity your own by doing as much or as little as you have time for!

1. **Print off** a copy of the two-page Advent House for each of your children. One copy is included in your book on pages 84–85, but it can also be found at www.myhelpclubformoms.com. Glue (or tape on the backside) the two pages together where they overlap, to form one large picture for your children to color. You may need to cut a bit of excess paper to allow both sides of the picture to line up just right.

2. **Gather markers** or crayons for your child to daily color the house.

3. **Purchase a bag of candy** so you can give your child a little sweet treat each day as you read the daily verse. God's Word is like honey on our lips, give your child a sweet taste for Scripture this Christmas! (Psalm 119:103)

4. **Look ahead at the daily activities** and decide if you would like to do any of them, and consider if you will need to gather any supplies.

5. **Now you are ready to begin!**

Read: On December 1st (or even the day before if you would prefer), read the following introductory paragraphs to your child:

> Today is the day! The first day of Advent! Can you believe Christmas is almost here? This is such a special time of year! Have you ever seen a Christmas gingerbread house, decorated with all sorts of delicious candy, sparkling with sugar and almost glowing with all of the excitement of Christmas? Our souls are just like a house too, a spectacular mansion with lots of rooms. But each of these rooms in our house is empty, just waiting to be filled, and it is up to you to decide how you will fill them!

> Now, I must tell you about your most amazing heavenly Father who loves you so much! He loves you enough to send His Son to rescue you from your sin and invites

you to follow Jesus and live with Him forever! This loving Father desires that you fill the rooms in your house with His beautiful treasures. Proverbs 24:3-4 tells us that "By wisdom a house is built, through knowledge it's rooms are filled with rare and beautiful treasures." In order to fill the rooms of your house with the treasures of the Lord, you must seek wisdom! And guess where wisdom is found? The Bible! As you read God's Word, His love letter to you, you fill each room in the house of your soul with the most lovely treasures imaginable! Treasures that shine with love, joy, peace, patience, kindness, goodness and faith!

This Christmas, as much as you are drawn to all of the decorations and presents, I want to encourage your heart to seek Jesus and learn to love His Word too! Jesus loves you so very much, you are His precious child and He wants you to seek Him this Christmas and every day throughout the year! So, each day for the next twenty-five days, we will read a few words from the Bible and you can color in a room from your Christmas house. All of these rooms are filled with the true treasures of Christmas! As you color each picture, I want you to think of the love God has for you and how He has many amazing treasures in store for you to find in Him!

Activity Instructions:

- **Day 1**: **Read Revelation 5:11-13**

  This may seem like a strange place to begin the Christmas story, but it is indeed the best place to start! From the time of the Garden of Eden when sin entered the world until now, there has been no one who could save us from our sins and from death. We needed a Rescuer! We needed God to bring us back into a right relationship with Him. And God loves us so much that He always had a plan to save us! He came to earth as a baby, like a precious, perfect little Lamb. He grew into a man, a man who never committed a single wrong and gave His life for us so that our soul, that which makes us who we are, would be able to live with Him forever, even after our body dies. In these verses we just read, angels and other creatures are praising Jesus, singing that He is God and is the only one worthy to receive honor, glory, power and strength forever and ever. Now that's what Christmas is all about! We, like the angels, are given an opportunity to live our lives with the purpose of loving and serving Jesus! What a priceless treasure we have been given! As we learn about the Christmas story over the next few weeks, keep in mind that this isn't just a story, but a gift that will change your whole life!

  Activity: Think about a gift that you would like to give to Jesus this Christmas. It could be desiring to talk to Him more, committing to read the Bible and learn more about Him, treating your brothers or sisters with kindness, telling others about Jesus, having a heart of thankfulness, or anything else! Find an old box or bag to decorate as your Jesus gift box. Over the next few days, when you decide what you want your gift to Jesus to be, write it on a paper, place it in the box and talk to Him about it. Let the Lord know how you would like to follow Him more closely this Christmas!

- **Day 2**: **Read Malachi 4:5**

  Let's go back in time, several hundred years before Jesus was born. God gave prophets, like Elijah, to prepare people's hearts for the coming of Jesus! He wanted people to have every opportunity to believe in the coming Messiah, the Savior who would wash away the sins of all who chose Him. Even now, He lovingly holds His children, washes away our sins, and offers us the opportunity to have a relationship, a friendship with Him that is closer than any other we could ever imagine. And guess what, He will be coming again soon to make all things right and bring us to heaven with Him, are you ready?

  Activity: Make a megaphone out of a paper towel or toilet paper tube. Jesus' first coming, His plan to rescue us and give us the opportunity to be saved from our sins is the reason we celebrate

Christmas! What a wonderful thing to be celebrating! And He will be coming again soon! Use your megaphone to announce the good news of Jesus to all who will listen! Celebrate today!

- **Day 3: Read Luke 1:11-20**

  Zechariah and his wife were very old when God sent an angel to tell him that his wife would have a baby—a very special baby who would prepare the way for Jesus! With God all things are possible! However, Zechariah didn't believe that God could do such a miracle in his life. What happened to Zechariah because of his unbelief?

  Activity: Write several words on slips of paper (animals, sports, or stories your children love work well). Have your child choose a slip of paper and act out what is written for others to guess. Is it more difficult to communicate when you cannot speak? How do you think Zechariah felt?

- **Day 4: Read Isaiah 7:14**

  Immanuel means "God with us." Can you believe that more than 700 years before Jesus was born, God sent a prophet to tell people that He would be sending a Rescuer, literally God in the form of a human to save all those who love Him? God has been planning your rescue from the time sin entered the world! He loves you so much!

  Activity: On a piece of paper, with permanent marker, write Immanuel in Hebrew (צמנואל) and its meaning, "God with us." He is eternal! Decorate the page with watercolor paints or any art supplies you have on hand!

- **Day 5: Read Luke 1:26-38**

  Mary was visited by an angel with some amazing news! What was it? Close your eyes and imagine being visited by an angel and receiving news such as what Mary received. How do you think Mary felt? Did you notice how she responded "I am the Lord's servant"? God is calling you to serve Him today too! He loves you so much! How can you serve the Lord as Mary did?

  Activity: Set out craft supplies for your child to make and decorate an angel. Let them be creative and design their own idea of how an angel may look. Keep it simple by providing just paper and crayons or add more supplies like feathers, glitter, sequins, yarn, cotton balls or scraps of construction paper or fabric.

- **Day 6: Free Day!**

- **Day 7: Free Day!**

- **Day 8: Read Luke 1:39-45**

  Even before John was born, he was able to recognize his Savior Jesus! Babies are amazing and are so precious to God from the very day they begin growing in their mother's belly!

  Activity: Look at ultrasound or newborn pictures of your child with him or her. Discuss how God made each baby special and valuable. Refer to Psalm 139:13-18 for a beautiful passage about how God forms each baby in his mother's womb. Talk to your children about how important it is to value babies as God's special creation!

- **Day 9: Read Luke 1:46-49**

  In these verses, Mary is praising God for the amazing gift He had given not only to her, but to the whole world as well! She had many reasons to be afraid of what this miraculous pregnancy would mean for her, but she chose to trust God and praise Him! Can you think of any situations in which you can trust God in a deeper way? How can you choose to live a life of praise before God too?

  Activity: Tape a piece of paper to the refrigerator or a wall and make a list throughout the day of things you can praise God for! Building a heart of praise from a young age is such a beautiful thing!

- **Day 10**: Read Luke 1:57-64

Elizabeth and Zechariah's baby was born! What did they name him? When John was grown, he had a very special job of spreading the glorious news that Jesus had come, God in the flesh, the Savior of all mankind! How can you spread the good news of our Savior Jesus this Christmas?

Activity: Make a Christmas card for someone to tell them about Jesus. You can even incorporate the following verse into your card to share the amazing news of Jesus. John 3:16, "For God so loved the world that he gave his one and only Son, that whoever believes in him shall not perish but have eternal life."

- **Day 11**: Read John 1:14

What a beautiful verse! This passage is talking about Jesus and how He came to earth as a baby to save us from our sins and give us eternal life if we choose to trust in Him. Have you chosen to trust in Him?

Activity: Pray for people you know or those around the world who do not follow Jesus. God desires that all people will come to a saving knowledge of Him!

- **Day 12**: Read Matthew 1:20-21

What did the angel tell Joseph to name the baby? Jesus! The name Jesus means "Savior." It was given to our Lord because "He saves His people from their sins" (Matthew 1:21). What a beautiful name, one that will stir love in your heart and praise on your lips!

Activity: Make a Jesus decoration for your tree! Make this as simple or complex as you would like! Here are a couple ideas: Grab an unembellished bulb from your Christmas tree and some permanent markers. Let your child write Jesus' name on the bulb and decorate the bulb as they would like. Alternately, cut a circle out of construction paper, glue popsicle sticks in the shape of an "x" to make a manger for baby Jesus. In the upper portion of the "x," glue some dried grass cut from outdoors. Make a baby Jesus by cutting off about 1" from the end of a third popsicle stick, drawing a face on the upper portion and wrapping the lower portion in fabric or a kleenex for a blanket. Glue baby Jesus in the manger and add yarn or string to the top as a hanger before placing on your tree.

- **Day 13**: Free Day!

- **Day 14**: Free Day!

- **Day 15**: Read Matthew 1:24-25 (Disclaimer: The first part of verse 25 mentions the timing of Mary and Joseph consummating their marriage. If you don't want to discuss the meaning of this term, feel free to just read the ending of the verse). Joseph obeyed the Lord by doing exactly as the angel had commanded him! Do you ever struggle with obeying the Lord?

Activity: God has an amazing plan for your life! Pray and ask the Lord to help you obey Him! Talk with your parents about an area in which you struggle to obey. Did you know that even parents have to obey God, and they understand how challenging obedience can be! Your mom and dad can help and encourage you as you grow to follow Jesus! With their help, write out or illustrate a plan for obeying God in the area in which you struggle.

- **Day 16**: Read Micah 5:2

Where did this verse say Jesus would be born? This prophecy was written several hundred years before Jesus was born. God orchestrated all the events surrounding Jesus birth (the census, Joseph and Mary's journey to Bethlehem, etc.) to make everything happen just as He had said it would! Our God is an awesome, all-knowing Father! He always does what He says He will!!

Activity: Sing the song "O Little Town of Bethlehem" together. You can even make musical instruments out of pots or pans and spoons to accompany your song.

- <u>Day 17</u>: Read Luke 2:1-5

  Jesus is about to be born! But Mary and Joseph must travel to Bethlehem for the census (counting the people from each town). Can you imagine traveling such a long distance riding on the back of a donkey? Or even walking alongside, as Joseph did, leading the donkey where he needed to go? They had to walk for several days to reach Bethlehem. They must have been tired!

  <u>Activity:</u> Let's pretend to be Mary and Joseph and take the journey ourselves! Go pack your bags, grab a donkey (an empty wrapping paper tube works well as a stick-donkey), and let's pretend to take the long walk to Bethlehem together!

- <u>Day 18</u>: Read Luke 2:8-15

  Imagine waking up in the middle of the night and looking up to see the sky full of angels praising God! Can you imagine what it must have been like? What a beautiful picture of how we should praise God forever more!

  <u>Activity:</u> Have a Shepherd's Meal and pretend you are a shepherd on the night of Jesus' birth! Instructions can be found in this book, just check out the table of contents!

- <u>Day 19</u>: Read Luke 2:6-7

  Our Savior is born! Praise the Lord for His great love for us! Let's say a prayer of thanksgiving for God's love and the way He takes care of us! He has provided a way for us to come back to Him and have a relationship with Him! What an amazing Father and what a wonderful Savior!

  <u>Activity:</u> Plan a birthday party for Jesus for sometime this week! Instructions can be found in this book (check out the table of contents). Let your child make some decorations for the party today. Just provide paper and markers and let them go at it! They can make a paper banner or even snowflakes to hang up for the party.

- <u>Day 20</u>: Free Day!

- <u>Day 21</u>: Free Day!

- <u>Day 22</u>: Read Matthew 1:24-25

  Jesus says that He is the light of the world. As we walk with Him, we do not have to live in darkness any longer! Each area of our lives can be flooded with His beautiful, glorious light! How can you choose to walk in that light today? How can you shine the light of Jesus to others around you?

  <u>Activity:</u> Light some candles and see how the room is bathed in a peaceful glow. How much more powerful and beautiful is the light of Jesus? Sing some Christmas carols together by candlelight and worship Jesus! Some ideas for carols include "Joy to the World," "O Holy Night," "Angels We Have Heard on High," and "Silent Night."

- <u>Day 23</u>: Read Philippians 2:6-11

  What a beautiful gift God has given us by coming to earth, taking the form of a man, suffering on the cross and dying so that we can live with Him forever! He loves you so very much! Have you chosen to follow Him? "Salvation is to be found through him alone; in all the world there is no one else whom God has given who can save us" (Acts 4:12 GNT).

  <u>Activity:</u> We have so much to thank Jesus for! Pray together and thank Him for rescuing us! We want to remember the true meaning of Christmas today and every day! To help your children really solidify the story of Jesus birth, bring it into their playtime by acting out the nativity story. In this book, we have provided more ideas on how to help your children act out the story, just check out the table of contents!

- <u>Day 24</u>: **Read 2 Peter 3:18**

  God has called us not just to believe that Jesus is real, but to grow in Him as well! We are called to follow Jesus and grow in Him every day we are alive on this earth. Jesus loves you so much that taking the journey of growing in Him is sure to be a fantastic adventure! What an exciting purpose God has given to you!

  <u>Activity:</u> On a piece of paper, draw a square flower pot with a green stem coming from the pot. Next, trace a few of your child's handprints in green on either side of the stem. This is their growing vine! Read John 15:5 and help your child come up with ways they can grow in their relationship with Jesus and stay connected to Him. Write those ideas on each traced handprint. Let your child color their vine and be reminded of how they can grow in their relationship with Jesus!

- <u>Day 25</u>: **Read Matthew 2:1-12**

  The Wisemen searched for Jesus because they wanted so badly to worship Him! Do you want to live life as the Wisemen did: giving everything and going any distance just to worship our Savior Jesus? I know I sure do!

  <u>Activity:</u> Take some time between the busy activities of Christmas Day to worship Jesus as a family. Talk about Him, pray together, sing songs of praise, read His Word…just do whatever God puts on your heart! Merry Christmas! What a perfect day to celebrate the Love of Jesus!

- <u>Optional activities for older children:</u>

  Some of the daily activities listed work best for younger children. If you would like to include activities this month for your older children, below are some ideas they may find enjoyable!

  1. Make a newspaper to document some of the events happening in the daily Scripture readings. Let them give their newspaper a fun name like "The Bethlehem Times" and add news stories, advertisements, and illustrations as they see fit. They can add to it a little bit at a time as something from a Scripture passage strikes their fancy.

  2. Write a poem or song of praise to the Lord. This is something they could work on through the month as God lays words of praise on their heart. When they are finished, type their creation out and place it in a frame to add as a precious memory to your Christmas decor. You can even have a family Christmas performance night in which everyone shares their creations if you are so inclined.

  3. Create a salt dough model or diorama in a shoe box or box lid (there are many great salt dough recipes online). Your child can make it in the form of the Nativity scene or perhaps a map of the journey that Mary and Joseph took even including their flight to Egypt after the birth of Jesus to escape Herod. Let them be creative; the sky's the limit!

  4. Have your child write a script to act out the story surrounding Jesus' birth. Write it screen-play style with different parts and exciting lines. Costumes and props can even be made by your child too!

  5. Staple several sheets of paper together to make a Christmas book detailing the events of the story of Jesus' birth. Each page can be written and illustrated by your child and can be read year after year to remember why we celebrate Christmas!

~Christmas~
~ Week Two ~

Dear Mom,

There is a favorite song of mine that I listen to every Christmas season by a country artist, and the main chorus of the song says, "A baby changes everything." The message is so simple, yet so profound! Jesus' entrance into this world as a precious baby, humbled and helpless, was the opposite of what everyone thought would happen as they awaited their Savior. They expected a mighty King, a great army to follow, and maybe even a grand feast to celebrate it all. But this small baby would change the world!

As you consider how to celebrate Christmas this year, I encourage you to keep the holiday simple—simply focused on Jesus, celebrating simply with family, and giving simple gifts. Everything you do doesn't have to be grand. Take Jesus' humble beginnings as an example of how to celebrate His birth.

With love,

Krystle Porter and the Help Club For Moms Team

" She will give birth to a son, and you are to give him the name Jesus, because he will save his people from their sins. "

~ Matthew 1:21

Mom Tips

By: Leslie Leonard

"For to us a child is born, to us a son is given, and the government will be on his shoulders. And he will be called Wonderful Counselor, Mighty God, Everlasting Father, Prince of Peace." ~ Isaiah 9:6

The Wise Woman Builds Her Spirit

- Think of a Christmas hymn that touches your heart. Print or write out the lyrics, and read them after your quiet time one or two days this week.
- Search for a Bible passage that echoes the hymn lyrics and write it in your journal. You will have a richer experience whenever you hear the song, knowing its scriptural connection.

The Wise Woman Loves Her Husband

- Start a yearly tradition just for you and your husband. Plan a quiet or festive date night, and make it a priority. Here are some simple ideas: go out for dessert or tea and take the long way home to enjoy Christmas lights; bundle up for a walk in the snow that ends with a snowball fight, or go ice skating.
- Find ways to pamper your husband this month. Greet him after work with a hot cup of cocoa, set aside extra Christmas cookies just for him, write him a heartfelt Christmas card, or just remember to pause the Christmas preparations to give him a smile and a big kiss.

The Wise Woman Loves Her Children

- Decorate sugar cookies with your kids this week. Here's a decorating tip: Instead of using flour to dust the counter to roll out your dough, which can leave sugar cookies bland on the outside, use powdered sugar instead! It easily dissolves into the dough without leaving a dusty residue.
- Involve your children in gift wrapping! They can make handmade gift tags from last year's Christmas cards, paper, stickers, markers, paint, natural objects, photos, etc. Set up a station with all the supplies they need to bring their ideas to life.

The Wise Woman Cares For Her Home

- Using pretty jars or containers and a tray, set up a Hot Cocoa Station on your counter. Include all of your hot chocolate fixings—cocoa, marshmallows, candy canes, shaved chocolate, as well as seasonal mugs, stirring straws or spoons.
- Prepare extra holiday food in advance to be frozen until your house guests arrive. Homemade bread, cinnamon rolls, and quick breads freeze well. Then, all you need to do is thaw them the night before and warm them up in the oven the next morning.

> "Glory to God in the highest heaven, and on earth peace to those on whom his favor rests."
>
> ~ Luke 2:14

> *"A great many people are trying to make peace, but that has already been done. God has not left it for us to do; all we have to do—is to enter into it."*
>
> ~ D.L Moody

- Good morning friend! Remember to call your prayer partner today. In the midst of the holiday season, it is so important to keep praying with one another. Now is a time when most of us need extra prayer to get through the stress and busyness, so don't give up!

- Jesus is the Prince of Peace, and he longs for you to enter into His eternal rest today. Pray for His Spirit to bring you fresh revelation as you pour over His Word.

- Open your Bible and read Luke 2:8-20. Write verse 14 in your journal along with the meaning of peace/shalom (below in the devotional).

The Shalom Peace of Jesus

By: Mari Jo Mast

Peace. Do you long for spiritual rest today?

When the angels announced the birth of Jesus to the shepherds, they were praising God and saying peace had come to earth. What could they possibly have known that caused them to rejoice so greatly? History tells us there was much political unrest and fear in the Jewish world at the time. So why rejoice, and what did it signify?

The Hebrew word for "peace" is shalom. Its deepest definition is "the spiritual harmony brought by an individual's restoration with God." The peace Jesus came to bring wasn't what the world, including the shepherds, were looking for at the time. Physical safety and political harmony were a longing and a priority, but not necessarily an immediate result of His birth. This was why they were disappointed and didn't recognize Jesus, yet the purpose of His birth was far greater. The true reason why Jesus came was to bring salvation and peace between us and God! The sacrifice of His life on the cross became a bridge between our ugly sin and a Holy God. His resurrection made the Holy Spirit available—bringing us eternal peace!

Hallelujah! What a Savior! Saying "yes" to Jesus brings us rest: rest from our own works, rest from our sin, rest from anxiety, anger, and depression, rest from obligations, rest in our relationship with Him and with others, and even rest from spiritual striving! This is the true meaning of peace. Jesus paid it all.

How we desperately need Him today. As it was 2,000 years ago, so it is now. There is much political unrest and confusion all around, yet we can access personal tranquility, right smack dab in the middle of all the chaos! Is your heart frenzied with all the holiday fuss? Does our current world situation bring you fear and unrest? Take a deep breath; there is hope. God has already provided!

Rejoice! You can be the embodiment of peace as you access Jesus by letting Him reign in you through His Spirit. There is a place in our hearts that can be quieted by no one but Him. Pray with me today:

> Dear Jesus, I need Your peace. According to the Word of God, I believe You are the One who brings perfect peace because You are the Prince of Peace (Isaiah 9:6)! I ask in Your name to calm and quiet my busy soul. Make my heart one with Yours. Help me keep my mind on you (Isaiah 26:3). Fill me to overflowing with Your Spirit, and bring eternal peace to my body, soul, and spirit. I receive and rejoice in the REST which only You can bring! Thank You for coming to make peace available. I celebrate You, I love You, and I am grateful for the gift of Your life to me. Amen.

Let the SHALOM of Christ rule in your heart!

Questions to Ponder:

- Ponder Isaiah 26:3: "You will keep Him in perfect peace, whose mind is stayed on You. Because He trusts in you." Ask the Holy Spirit to fill you to the brim and overflowing every day as you are aware of His presence, moment by moment. Tell Him you want more of Him and His truth. Make it your goal to submit your thoughts to His Spirit as you go about this busy holiday season.

- Think about it: Are your thoughts dwelling on Jesus and are you trusting Him? Write your pondering in your journal.

Faith-Filled Ideas:

As you pray for the peace of Jesus this Christmas, make every effort to keep peace in your own home. Become a peace-loving mom simply by being nice to your family. Try to avoid things or situations which may steal your peace and make you grouchy. When you get stressed, decompress with your favorite relaxing activity such as a long bubble bath, a walk outside in the brisk air, or simply a nap. Be sure to plan downtime and relaxation in your family's schedule, too.

Journal

_____

_____

_____

_____

_____

_____

_____

_____

_____

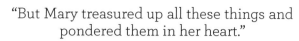

"But Mary treasured up all these things and
pondered them in her heart."

~ Luke 2:19

"When God reveals truth to you, by whatever means, that is a divine encounter."
~ Henry Blackaby

- Good morning! Grab your Bible, a pen, and your journal, and find a cozy place to sit. It's time to meet with your Savior!
- Read Luke 2:8-20. Write verse 19 in your journal. If you haven't done so this December, I encourage you to take some time to read all of Luke 1 and 2.

Believe and Ponder

By: Jennifer Valdois

I love the Christmas song, "Mary Did You Know?" by Mark Lowry. This song asks powerful questions of young Mary, chosen by God to carry His Son. Did she realize that when she kissed her little baby, she was kissing the face of God? Or that the sleeping child she was holding was the great I Am?

I want to learn to be more like Mary. She was quick to believe God, and she quietly pondered the things of God in her heart.

In Luke chapter one, we first read about Zechariah doubting the angel who told him his barren wife would bear a child. Then, we read about Mary. An angel appears to her and tells her she will conceive by the Holy Spirit and give birth to the Son of God. Amazingly, Mary believes God right away. She says, "I am the Lord's servant, may it be to me as you have said" (Luke 1:38 NLT).

Don't you want to be like Mary and take God at His word? When we read the Bible, God speaks to us. He tells us we are His and He guides us into all truth.

> All scripture is God breathed and is useful for teaching, rebuking, correcting and training in righteousness, so that the servant of God may be thoroughly equipped for every good work. (2 Timothy 3:16-17)

What is He saying to you today during this Christmas season? Above all, I hope you hear that you are dearly loved. He sent His only begotten Son so you may live with Him forever.

In Luke chapter two, the angel of the Lord returns, appearing to shepherds and announcing the birth of the promised Savior. After the shepherds find Mary, Joseph, and Jesus, they tell everyone they know what they have seen and heard. In contrast, the Bible says, "Mary treasured up all these things and pondered them in her heart" (Luke 2:19).

Incredible things were happening before her very eyes, yet she did not run around telling everyone she knew. Rather, she tucked them away—even the things she didn't understand—and pondered them in her heart.

I want to be more introspective like Mary and meditate on the things of God. As I witness answered prayers and blessings all around me, I want to remember them, pondering God's goodness and treasuring them in my heart. It is my prayer that these thoughts will spill over into what I say and do. All too often, my words can be harsh, and I say things I regret. I need the power of God operating in my life so I can be "quick to listen, slow to speak, and slow to become angry" (James 1:19).

Please pray with me this Christmas season:

Jesus, help me to be more like Mary and believe in God's Word and His promises. Help me to treasure the things of God in my heart.

Questions to Ponder:

- Take some time to remember some of the amazing things God did in your life this year and write them in your journal. How did God answer your prayers?

- Are you believing God for something specific? Find a promise in Scripture to which you can cling. Write the Scripture on an index card and place it where you will see it throughout the day. Focus on believing God and taking Him at His Word.

Faith-Filled Ideas:

Teach your children the joy of generosity by giving gifts to those less fortunate.

Our favorite Christmas activity is packing shoebox gifts for Operation Christmas Child. Samaritan's Purse delivers the gift-filled shoeboxes to children around the world who would otherwise never receive a gift. These gifts have the power to transform the lives of children and their families through the Good News of Jesus Christ! Our love for this ministry and the children grows each year!

How to Pack a Shoebox:

Start with an average-sized shoebox. Decide if you will pack for a boy or a girl. Choose from three age categories ranging from 2 to 14 years old. Fill the box with gifts! Start with something the child will love like a stuffed animal, doll, toy truck, or ball with a pump. Next, fill it with school supplies, non-liquid hygiene items, and accessories like underwear or socks. These items we take for granted may be the most exciting part of the gift!

I shop for items to pack throughout the year. I look for sweet stuffed animals and other fun toys on sale after the holidays. I shop with coupons for toothbrushes, and I buy all the school supplies when they are marked down during the back to school sales. You can also make your dollar stretch by buying large packages of socks, underwear, washcloths, combs, bar soap, etc., and dividing them amongst the boxes you pack.

I love the impact Operation Christmas Child has on my children. My daughter tells me over and over, "It makes me feel so good to pack OCC shoeboxes. It makes me feel good to help kids who don't have anything." We live an hour away from an Operation Christmas Child Distribution Center. Now that my children are old enough, we have started volunteering to inspect the shoeboxes. It is an incredible way to encourage and teach our children to serve!

Go to www.samaritanspurse.org for more information on how to send a shoebox for a child in need.

journal

> "'Martha, Martha,' the Lord answered,
> 'you are worried and upset about many things, but
> only one thing is needed. Mary has chosen what is better,
> and it will not be taken away from her.'"
>
> ~ Luke 10:41-42

"Things which matter most must never be at the mercy of things which matter least."

~ Johann Wolfgang von Goethe

- Find a quiet place to spend time with Jesus. Silence your phone, take a deep breath, and clear your mind of everything else.
- Read Luke 10:38-42. Write Luke 10:41-42 in your journal, and underline the first half of verse 42: "...but few things are needed—or indeed only one."

Only One Thing Is Needed

By: Heather Doolittle

You know the story of Martha and Mary, the one where Martha is doing all the work, Mary is sitting around chatting with Jesus, and then Jesus tells Martha that Mary is the one doing the good thing? Really?! If I were Martha, I might have had a good laugh before realizing He was being serious.

Imagine staying up half the night cleaning before your in-laws arrive, but your husband opts to go to bed early, leaving you with the extra work. By morning, the house is spotless, your husband is cheerful and refreshed, but you're mildly cranky and completely exhausted. Your in-laws show up, compare you to your fresh-faced husband, and rebuke you for not being more like him! After all your hard work! I would be indignant! But isn't that what Jesus did? He told his well-intentioned friend, "Martha, Martha...you are worried and upset about many things, but few things are needed—or indeed only one. Mary has chosen what is better, and it will not be taken away from her" (Luke 10:41-42).

Jesus knew Martha's heart; He knew exactly what she needed. Jesus was not being unkind or ungrateful, but compassionate. He was releasing Martha from her mundane earthly burdens and giving his dear friend an invitation to rest and enjoy His peace. You are Jesus' dearly loved friend, too. He has not called you to be a workhorse, bearing all that you possibly can handle. Don't look to the world around you and take on burdens God never intended. Instead, take the time to sit at your Savior's feet, trusting Him to "establish the work of [your] hands," and make your best efforts fruitful (Psalm 90:17).

In just a couple of weeks, your clean house will be littered with presents and bows, your delicious dinner will be replaced by mounds of dirty dishes, and your beautiful decorations will return to their boxes. However, if you spend extra time with your God and with the people He has given you to love, that investment will never be taken away.

I love the words of Jesus as He urges us to:

> Come to me, all you who are weary and burdened, and I will give you rest. Take my yoke upon you and learn from me, for I am gentle and humble in heart, and you will find rest for your souls. For my yoke is easy and my burden is light. (Matthew 11:28-30)

Nourishing your soul and cultivating a relationship with Jesus is your first priority, not your last.

Are you drawing near to Jesus this season, finding rest for your soul, growing in gentleness and humility? Spend time in prayer and God's Word to find out what His plan is for your family in this season. He wants you to create Christmas memories to be cherished for years, and He can make it happen with ease. He is God. All He needs from you is your faithfulness, not 18-hour days of chaos nor every last dollar in your checking account. He knows exactly how to bless you and your family, but you first must let go of your plans and expectations in order to submit to His.

Questions to Ponder

- Are you taking time to sit at the feet of your Savior? If not, what is getting in the way? Pray that God will help you to overcome any obstacles that are robbing you of your peace or your time with Jesus.

- Prayerfully plan daily quiet time with God. See where it fits into your schedule. Set an alarm if you need to, or plan a 30-minute show or activity for you children. Be intentional about silencing distractions or interruptions.

Faith-Filled Ideas

What if you did things differently this year? Lower your standards a bit, re-prioritize your tasks, put Jesus and relationships first, and ignore everything else. Delegate. Make cooking and cleaning a family affair. Praise and reward everyone for completing the tasks together. Lay your burdens and expectations at the cross in order to make December a month of living like God's chosen people. Live like someone who is holy and dearly loved, someone whose primary purpose is to love God and help those around you to do the same.

Here's an idea. We're about halfway between Thanksgiving and Christmas. If you're like me, your to-do list is still a mile long. Now is a great time to examine your goals and priorities to make sure you are focusing on what matters most. If you haven't spent time with Jesus or taught your children about our Savior, start now. This is what I want you to do:

- Write a list of everything you have to do before Christmas.

- Examine each item to determine what your underlying motivation is. Perfection? Pride? Who are you really serving: your Savior, your guests, or yourself?

- Cross everything off your list that does not serve Jesus or bring His peace and joy to your home. Does the house really have to be spotless?

- Can you pare down your Christmas menu or buy a pie from a store this year? Let your children and husband wrap the gifts and accept that they may not look great.

- Replace each of the extraneous tasks you just crossed off with soul-filling quiet time or family time. You may be able or tempted to squeeze those extra crossed-off tasks into your downtime, but don't do it! God was speaking to you, telling you how to find rest. Fill that time with something eternal.

journal

_____

_____

_____

_____

_____

_____

_____

_____

_____

_____

_____

_____

_____

_____

_____

_____

_____

_____

_____

_____

_____

_____

_____

_____

_____

_____

_____

_____

_____

_____

Christmas ~ Week Two

My husband had the sweetest grandmother I have ever known! Mona Weakly loved the Lord and loved people. I frequently received hand-written letters in the most beautiful cursive I have ever seen! She wrote of her simple life and what was happening in her world with such love and care. She loved me like I was her own granddaughter.

Grandma Weakly, as we called her, was an incredible cook, always ready with fresh-baked cookies on hand for visitors. She ate sugar every single day and somehow managed to stay thin and live to be 95 years old! Her Pumpkin Pie recipe is the most delicious I have ever had in my life, and the crust is super simple. I can't wait to see Grandma in heaven someday to give her a big hug!

GRANDMA WEAKLY'S PUMPKIN PIE

By: Deb Weakly & Mona Weakly

Ingredients

1 large can (29 oz) Libby's Pumpkin

3 cups sugar

4 eggs

1 ½ Tbsp cinnamon

½ tsp salt

3 Tbsp flour

1 large can evaporated milk (12 oz)

½ cup milk

2 Tbsp half and half

Directions:

1. Preheat oven to 400 degrees.

2. Beat eggs until fluffy.

3. Add remaining ingredients.

4. Pour into Grandma's **Press-in-the-Pan Pie Crust** (see recipe on the next page).

5. Bake at 400 degrees for 15 minutes then lower the oven temperature to 325 degrees for 45 minutes.

6. Cool before eating.

Food for the Soul

GRANDMA WEAKLY'S PUMPKIN PIE

By: Deb Weakly & Mona Weakly

PRESS-IN-THE-PAN PIE CRUST

Ingredients

- 1 ½ cup flour
- 1 tsp salt
- 1 Tbsp sugar
- ½ cup oil
- 2 Tbsp milk or half and half

Directions:

1. Mix well and press thinly into the pie pan.

2. Pre-bake in pre-heated oven for 5 minutes at 400 degrees.

3. Add filling and continue to bake the pie according to directions.

～ COOL ～
Christmas Science!

By: Tara Davis

Fun Christmas Science Projects that Point to Jesus!

1. Jesus Gives Living Water

> Jesus stood up and cried out, "If anyone thirsts, let him come to me and drink. Whoever believes in me, as the Scripture has said, 'Out of his heart will flow rivers of living water.'" Now this he said about the Spirit, whom those who believed in him were to receive. (John 7:37-39 ESV)

We celebrate Jesus' birth at Christmas because He came to bring us life! When we choose to follow Him, He fills us with Living Water—the Holy Spirit—and we will never be the same again!

Materials:

- Two balloons
- Candle flame
- Water

Demonstration:

1. Fill a balloon ¾ full with water. Blow air to fill it all the way.

2. Blow up the second balloon without water.

3. Place the flame of a lit candle on the part of the balloon filled with water and see what happens. As long as you put the flame on the part filled with water, nothing will happen. Water, a great conductor of heat, will not allow the balloon rubber to overheat and be destroyed.

4. Now place the flame on the second balloon without water and see what happens. It will pop as the unprotected rubber is destroyed by the flame.

Discuss:

Jesus came to rescue us! He died on the cross to forgive us of our sins, rose from the dead, and later returned back to heaven. He didn't leave us alone though! He left us the Holy Spirit who is Living Water for our souls. He protects us from the destructive "flames" of the hurts that come from living in this world. Although we may experience bullies at school, friends who hurt our feelings, or unfair situations, we will not be destroyed because our identity and worth is in Christ! He tells you who you are, a child of the living God, not a child of the world! Greater is He who is in you (Jesus) than He who is in the world (1 John 4:4 paraphrase).

~COOL~
Christmas Science!

By: Tara Davis

Fun Christmas Science Projects that Point to Jesus!

2. Candy Canes and Jesus

"For unto you is born this day in the city of David a Savior, who is Christ the Lord" (Luke 2:11 KJV).

We see candy canes everywhere at Christmastime. These sweet treats were designed to represent the Savior. Check out this little poem to see how, and then grab a couple for a demonstration to teach about how Jesus works in our lives!

Look at the Candy Cane
What do you see?
Stripes that are red
Like the blood shed for me
White is for my Savior
Who's sinless and pure!
"J" is for Jesus My Lord, that's for sure!
Turn it around
And a staff you will see
Jesus my shepherd
Was born for Me!

~ (author unknown)

Demonstration:

1. Lay a candy cane on a white plate or dish filled with room temperature water (enough water to cover about half the height of the candy cane).

2. As the minutes tick by, the warm water will dissolve the sugar of the candy cane, and you will see the red food coloring spread across the plate.

Discuss:

When we follow Jesus as our Savior, ask Him to forgive us, and allow Him to fill us with the Living Water of the Holy Spirit, we will begin to spread the love of Christ to everyone around us! Just as in the poem above, the red of the candy cane stands for the blood shed by Christ to forgive our sins. In this experiment, the red of the candy cane soaked in the "living water" can't help but spread in all directions. When we are filled with the Holy Spirit, we will not be able to contain the amazing news of Jesus' sacrifice for us! Pray that God will fill you with the full measure of His Spirit, and that He will give you opportunities to share about Him and His love to others!

Christmas

~ Week Three ~

Dear Mama,

How's your Christmas season going? Do you feel the stress and pressure starting to build as you are getting closer to Christmas with a list a mile long and not enough time in the day?

While out shopping, I noticed most everyone running here and there, obviously behind on their Christmas lists, with hardly a smile or a kind word to spare. I found myself wondering why it always has to be so stressful at this time of year?

Christmas can be a delightful time in our lives, but it can also be an overwhelming and not so enjoyable season. Right about now it can feel like everything is falling on your shoulders—so much to do and way too much stress to add to an already overcrowded life.

Even in the midst of our busyness, do you hear the still small voice of Jesus calling you to come away with Him? He still says the beautiful words he spoke over 2000 years ago,

> Come to me, all you who are weary and burdened, and I will give you rest. Take my yoke upon you and learn from me, for I am gentle and humble in heart, and you will find rest for your souls. For my yoke is easy and my burden is light. (Matthew 11:29-30)

This Christmas season, make every effort to listen for the call of Jesus, every day, one day at a time, one hour at a time, one moment at a time.

Try these ideas to help you connect with Jesus during this busy time of year:

1. Plan to spend time in your Bible study each morning. If you are having difficulty getting up, ask God to wake you up 15 minutes earlier in the morning. Then, ask Him for energy for your day. He will wake you up and give you more energy! Trust me, He has done this for me many times before!

2. Make sure to start your day with prayer and commit your day and all of your tasks to God. Pray for wisdom, and the help you need to get everything done. Pray for bargains while Christmas shopping, and for Him to give you the time for each and every task. Ask Him to help you be patient with your family.

3. Ask Him to speak to you as you do the Help Club Bible studies, and make sure to write in your journal what stands out to you as you read. Record any verses you want to remember on your phone recording device and listen to them many times this week to stay encouraged!

4. Then go about your day, in the power of the Holy Spirit, knowing He will help you in all you need to do!

We are praying for you and hope you have a great week!

With love,

Deb and the Help Club For Moms Team

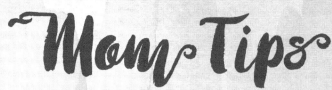

Mom Tips

By: Leslie Leonard

"For to us a child is born, to us a son is given, and the government will be on his shoulders. And he will be called Wonderful Counselor, Mighty God, Everlasting Father, Prince of Peace." ~ Isaiah 9:6

The Wise Woman Builds Her Spirit

- Give yourself permission to indulge in your favorite treats. You know you're going to do it anyway, so enjoy it! Just be selective, so you're not eating sweets purely out of convenience.
- Record Luke 2:9-14 on your phone recording device. Play this beautiful reminder over and over this week to remind you of the beautiful night our Savior was born!

The Wise Woman Loves Her Husband

- Make plans for you and your husband to attend a local church's Christmas program (just the two of you). Grab a coffee or dessert at your special place after the performance.
- Ask your husband what his favorite Christmas treat or tradition is, and make that a priority to do with him or for him.

The Wise Woman Loves Her Children

- Have a snowflake making contest. Even little ones can make simple snowflakes! See who can cut out the most detailed snowflake, the silliest, the most creative, the largest, the smallest, etc. Use the snowflakes to decorate windows in your home!
- Buy new matching pajamas for your kids to wear Christmas Eve. Everyone goes to bed with new, snuggly pajamas and you get adorable, coordinated pictures around the tree the next morning.

The Wise Woman Cares For Her Home

- Make your home smell like Christmas! In a pan of water on the stove top, place a combination of apples or oranges, cinnamon sticks, cloves, nutmeg, allspice, bay leaves, cranberries—whatever you have on hand. Your house will be smelling festive in no time!
- Spend some time with your children going through their toys, getting rid of the ones they no longer play with, and making room for their new ones. If the toys are in great condition and you have time, consider selling them on a trusted children's "buy and sell" Facebook page.

"Let us rejoice and be glad and give him glory!
For the wedding of the Lamb has come,
and his bride has made herself ready.
Fine linen, bright and clean, was given her to wear."

~ Revelation 19:7-9

"The most excellent method I have found for going to God is that of doing our common business without any view of pleasing men but purely for the love of God."
~ Brother Lawrence

- Call your prayer partner for your 10-minute prayer call! God is the one who has the power to work in your heart and the hearts of those you love. Prayer changes everything!
- Meet with your Beloved, your Betrothed. As you meditate on the following verses, bask in the love your Creator lavishes on you at every moment. Imagine Him singing over you, delighting in you, longing to make you His forever.
- Read verses Isaiah 54:5, Isaiah 62:3-5, Revelation 19:7-9, and Revelation 21:1-27.

Investing in Your Marriage

By: Christie Frieg

I know this title may sound odd, in light of the fact that we've been talking about Christmas for the past three weeks. Of course it's important to invest in your spouse any time of year, but today, I'm talking about your marriage to Christ.

Even though the ceremony will be held in the future, we are betrothed to Christ, our Beloved. In Jewish culture, betrothal is almost synonymous to marriage. This is the period of wooing and courtship.

Think of it this way: There we were, all alone, drifting, flitting from disappointment to empty disappointment, searching for meaning and purpose in all the wrong places. And yet, in every glorious sunset, every captivating landscape, every dazzling, star-filled night sky, our Beloved could be heard and seen—wooing us. In the ultimate gesture of sacrifice, He gave of His very self so that we could draw near to Him for all eternity, sharing in His love, joy, and beauty. And He draws us still, every day, every moment. He is closer than our skin, permeating our very being: always present, forever beckoning, gloriously loving.

So often, I hear worship songs in church and on the radio about how much God loves us. "Oh, how He loves us, how He loves us so!" There is no more wonderful truth in all the world than this.

But how many worship songs do we sing about our love for Him? For every stanza starring God's love toward us, are there even half as many regarding the depth of our love for Him?

I think not.

Suppose it is your anniversary. Your husband has spent weeks preparing the most wonderful day filled with fun, meaningful gestures. A visit to where you met, got engaged, or were married. A

Christmas ~ Week Three ~ Day One

trail of rose petals to a candlelit display with the words, "I love you now, always, and forever, with everything I am!" in giant letters in a painting he created himself. You can't believe how lucky you are, and you go to bed that night completely happy. But the next morning, when you wake up, you lean over and inform him, "Honey, I'm just not sure if I feel your love. I need to know you love me. It's hard to believe sometimes; I just need more faith to believe it." How would he respond?

Yet so often, we do that to our own Beloved. Instead of reciprocating or finding ways to bless Him, we may never get to a point where we enter into a two-way love relationship. We forget that He has committed His whole being to us, as it says in Hosea, "I will betroth you to me forever. I will betroth you to me in righteousness, and in justice, in steadfast love and in mercy" (Hosea 2:19). He is the most beautiful, kind, faithful, fun, and exciting husband we could ever have!

This Christmas, I challenge you to love your Husband. I challenge you to enter into a two-way relationship, and let God's demonstrations of love to you elicit an overflow of praise and love from your heart.

Questions to Ponder:

- What tasks do I perform every day that seem too ordinary to be pleasing to God? How can I adjust my mindset so that I can direct my efforts all to the glory of God, in even the smallest, most insignificant action?

- How can I cultivate a deep love toward Jesus? What could I incorporate into my Christmas season that would bring a smile to His face, effectively hanging a big banner that says, "I love you more than anything, with everything I am!"

Faith-Filled Ideas:

How do we reciprocate Christ's love for us? As Brother Lawrence said above, every little thing we do can be done solely for the love of God. Even though Brother Lawrence was the "janitor" of the monastery, it is quite possible that he served and loved God more than any other monk in the establishment. "I resolved to make the love of God the end of all my actions...I resolve even to take up a straw from the ground for the love of God, seeking Him only, and nothing else, not even His gifts." No piece of his daily routine was too mundane to be used for the glory and love of his dear Savior. So should it be with us.

It doesn't necessarily take extra time or grand gestures to love your Savior better. Talk to Him, consciously devoting your heart and your thoughts to Jesus throughout the day. You will begin to see His goodness in the mundane details of life and love Him more for it.

journal

_____

_____

_____

_____

_____

journal

> "Nevertheless I am continually with You;
> You have taken hold of my right hand. With your counsel
> You will guide me, and afterward receive me to glory."
>
> ~ Psalm 73:23-24 (NASB)

"Christmas can't be bought from a store...
Maybe Christmas means a little bit more."
~ Dr. Seuss

- Dear Mom, as we all lead busy lives with kids in tow, we need the gentle reminder that Jesus is truly the reason for the season!

- Read Luke 2:1-20. As you read the Christmas story, take it all in that Jesus came to us because we were in need of a Savior! Take a moment to praise Him!

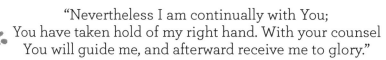

Partnering with God this Christmas

By: Krystle Porter

As I consider Christmas and realize that Christ is at the very center, it beckons me to refocus my lens and make sure that He is woven throughout all I strive to do during Christmastime.

I adore holidays, especially Christmas. In our home, we celebrate with decorations and fun activities, and there is a general joy of anticipating what's to come. I find though, that as my kids get older, I want to drown out all the "noise" of the holiday that keeps us engaged in the culture, and remember what we are really celebrating: Christ's entrance into this world as our Savior! Now don't get me wrong, I enjoy watching *Elf*, sipping hot chocolate, and making gingerbread houses as much as the next person, but if these take the place of honoring Jesus in my home (and they have some years!), my heart starts to feel heavy and uneasy.

In church one day, my pastor talked about "partnering with God" as we begin our day by saying, "Holy Spirit, help me today to partner with you in all I do." I wondered how I could draw near to God in the hustle and bustle of the Christmas season. During the holidays, God gets lost in the never-ending to-do list. At times, my to-do list to create a perfect celebration trumps the celebration itself! I have it backwards!

What if I started my Christmas season in a quiet space, with my heart turned heavenward, asking expectantly, "God, how can I partner with you this Christmas? What activities and gifts will lead my family to experience your entrance into this world more fully? How can my heart be turned to you this season?"

As you ponder this idea, imagine you are taking God's hand and letting Him lead you this season. Push away feelings of measuring up, buying the perfect gifts, or setting the most impressive table. Set your eyes on Christ this Christmas, and as you partner with Him, His presence will bless your family with joy!

Christmas ~ Week Three

"Nevertheless I am continually with You; You have taken hold of my right hand. With your counsel You will guide me, And afterward receive me to glory" (Psalm 73:23-24).

Questions to Ponder:

- What does a typical Christmas look like for you? Are you pleased with your approach or is there something you could change?

- What would a Christ-centered Christmas look like to you, ideally? Take people-pleasing off of the table! If there were no expectations from others, what would your ideal Christmas look like?

Faith-Filled Ideas:

Read Proverbs 3:5-6. Instead of your normal to-do list for the season, make a CHRIST-centered to-do list! Plan a special, set apart time to pray and consider what God would have you do in your home this season for Him! Who can you bless this season? Is there a family in need that you can help? What type of gifts is God calling you to give? Does He want you to give lavishly to someone, or is He telling you to give of yourself in some way? God will speak to your heart, but remember to write it all down!

Journal

_____

_____

_____

_____

_____

_____

_____

_____

_____

_____

_____

_____

_____

_____

_____

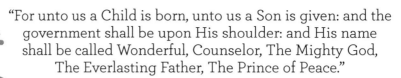

> "For unto us a Child is born, unto us a Son is given: and the
> government shall be upon His shoulder: and His name
> shall be called Wonderful, Counselor, The Mighty God,
> The Everlasting Father, The Prince of Peace."
>
> ~ Isaiah 9:6 (KJV)

"Christmas is a love story worth celebrating: A Savior, giving up all strength to come down to earth as a baby, to save His beloved."

- With your Bible in hand, find a comfortable spot to have your quiet time with Jesus. Pray that the Lord will bring peace to your spirit and speak to you today.

- Read and meditate on Luke 2:1-21. Write the verse that most stands out to you in your journal.

A Savior Worth Celebrating

By: Tara Davis

My sweet friend, I know you have been trying so hard. Sometimes the weight of Christmas pulls at us, unleashing such pressure to perform, to live up to the expectations of others, to create a magical season for those around us. We lose our peace; we let go of our focus. We set our sights on making it through the holidays. What if it were different? What if Jesus could remain our family's focal point, our reason for celebrating?

What an amazing gift we were given that night over two thousand years ago! Since the birth of sin into the world, humanity had been struggling. People had been consumed by the weight of sin, living in a world wrapped in darkness and self-inflicted sadness. We never could have saved ourselves from *ourselves*. However, God had a plan! We needed a Savior, a Messiah. We needed Jesus.

Our King came, not with strength and power, but as a weak, vulnerable babe. Because of this, He understands our weakness; He knows what kind of love we need. Hebrews 5:2 reveals that, "He is able to deal gently with those who are ignorant and are going astray, since He himself is subject to weakness." We can celebrate His tender understanding for each of His precious children!

Out of His great love for us, Jesus took on flesh. Ephesians 1:4 (ASV) whispers encouragement to our hearts, "...he chose us in him before the foundation of the world, that we should be holy and without blemish before him in love." Christmas is a love story worth celebrating: A Savior, giving up all strength to come down to earth as a baby, to save His beloved. We can celebrate Him because of His loving desire for us!

During His life on earth, Jesus went to impossible lengths to rescue us. As we grasp onto Him, He holds us and never lets us go. He is the love that never ends, the essence of hope, the restorer of peace, the giver of joy. He is "Immanuel, which means God with us" (Matthew 1:23). We can find peace in Whom we are now able to belong. We celebrate Him because of who He is and His undeniable adoration for us!

He was born for YOU, dear sister! The Lord is abounding in steadfast love for YOU (Psalm 86:15)! He is the only one who can bring you peace, who can understand your heart, and who can love you as only a Savior is able. This week we will be given the honor of celebrating Him! He is absolutely worthy of every single ounce of praise we are able to offer!

Questions to Ponder:

- Are you feeling worn out by Christmas preparations? Take a moment to ask the Lord to renew your focus on Jesus this week. He loves when we come to Him and is always willing to guide us back to His love!

- Think of one thing you can do to bring glory to Jesus this week. Can you commit to spending time with Him everyday, even though your days are busy? Maybe you can plan a special time with your family to truly praise the Lord for the amazing gift of Jesus.

Faith-Filled Ideas:

Would you like to celebrate Jesus in a memorable way this Christmas? This celebration can take place on Christmas Day or in the days prior. You can choose to do as much or as little as you want. Do not let the addition of a Jesus Celebration bring any additional weight to your Christmas, and do not feel pressured to make this celebration complicated or elaborate. Just do what works for you!

The following ideas serve as an example of a few ways to make your celebration special!

1. Read His Story: The Greatest Love Story Ever Told

It is important to share the story of our Savior on His birthday! There are many great versions of the story of Jesus' birth for children. I read out of the *Jesus Storybook Bible*. However, you could read straight from Luke chapter 2 as well! As you read, make sure to discuss any thoughts or questions your children have.

2. Every Party Needs a Cake!

Having a cake for Jesus is a fun way to celebrate! We made a cake with symbolic meaning (although picking up a cake from the grocery store would be just as delicious). No birthday celebration is complete without singing, "Happy Birthday!"

As you assemble and decorate your cake together, it is wonderful to share with your children why Jesus came. We decorate the cake as part of our celebration just before we cut and eat it! It is fun to let your children decorate as you talk about the cake's meaning! Remember, this cake does not need to be a Pinterest perfect cake! Your kids will have fun making it and the combination of Scripture, sugar, and fun will hopefully sink into their hearts in a deep, lasting way. The cake may end up looking like a pile of frosting, but, in the end, the sweet memories will be so worth it!

(Mom tip: If you do not have cake decorating supplies, simply fill a ziplock bag with your frosting, cut a small bit off one of the corners, and decorate away!)

** *If you would like to make a symbolic cake as well, an example of the symbols we used and their meanings can be found in Food for the Soul on the next page!*

3. **Sing Praises to the Newborn King!**
Join your children in worshipping our Savior with Christmas hymns. The angels, shepherds, and Wisemen worshipped baby Jesus, and we should as well! There are so many amazing Christ-honoring Christmas carols you can sing with your children. We praise the Lord with, "Away in a Manger" and "Joy to the World."

4. **Lay Your Gifts at His Feet**
We do a Jesus gift box each year in which we place gifts from our heart to our Savior. For a better explanation of how to do a Jesus gift box, be sure to watch Deb's video at: https://vimeo.com/149602537.

journal

_____

_____

_____

_____

_____

_____

_____

_____

_____

_____

_____

_____

_____

_____

_____

_____

_____

_____

_____

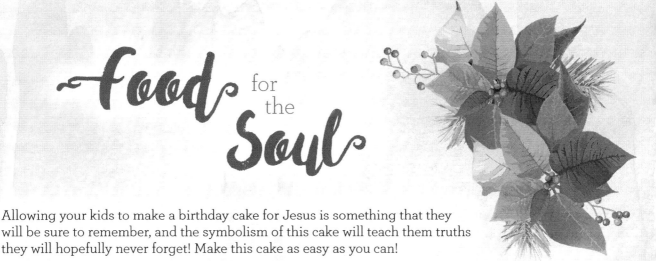

Food for the Soul

Allowing your kids to make a birthday cake for Jesus is something that they will be sure to remember, and the symbolism of this cake will teach them truths they will hopefully never forget! Make this cake as easy as you can!

Use cake mix or even buy a pre-made round chocolate cake with white frosting. Buy frosting already in tubes; or make it, place it in sandwich bags, and cut off the very tip of the bag to pipe it onto the cake. This cake is not going to be perfect and its beauty will be in the fact that your kids enjoyed making it together!

As you read each item of symbolism, pass the cake around the table and take turns adding the appropriate frosting decor to the cake!

You can also find additional details in the previous Bible study in Christmas Week Three – Day Three on page 108, *A Savior Worth Celebrating*.

BIRTHDAY CAKE FOR JESUS

By: Tara Davis

Symbolism:

- **Round Cake:** The shape of the cake is round with no end, showing that God's love is never-ending. He loves us so much that He sent His only Son to die for our sins (John 3:16).
- **Dark Cake:** Before knowing Jesus, our hearts are like this dark cake, and we cannot spend eternity with the Lord with hearts so full of sin (Romans 3:23).
- **White frosting:** God did a wonderful thing when He sent his son Jesus to die for our sins. Now all the darkness is covered up, and Jesus washes our sins white as snow. We are pure white in the sight of God. When we ask Jesus to forgive all the bad things we've done, we are white like this frosting (Romans 6:23).
- **Star:** The star reminds us of the star in Bethlehem and how the Wisemen followed it in order to worship the Lord Jesus. It reminds us that we should worship and follow Him every day.
- **Red candle:** The red color reminds us of Jesus' blood that was shed for the forgiveness of our sins. Because He died and rose again, we can have eternal life in heaven with Jesus if we believe in Him (Romans 5:8).
- **Light the Candle:** The glow of the candle reminds us that Jesus can shine in our hearts if we just ask Him to be our Savior (Matthew 5:16).
- **Evergreens:** Evergreens around the cake remind us of something living and always growing. If we have accepted Jesus to be the Savior of our lives, we are going to grow and get to know Him more. We can grow to know Him better by praying, talking about Him, reading our Bibles, and sharing Him with others (John 15:5 or 2 Peter 3:18).

10 Scriptures to Savor this Christmas

1. **2 Corinthians 9:15** – "Thanks be to God for His indescribable gift!"

2. **John 1:14** – "The Word became flesh and made His dwelling among us. We have seen His glory, the glory of the one and only Son, who came from the Father, full of grace and truth."

3. **Matthew 1:21** – "She will give birth to a son, and you are to give Him the name Jesus, because He will save His people from their sins."

4. **Romans 6:23** – "For the wages of sin is death, but the gift of God is eternal life in Christ Jesus our Lord."

5. **Galatians 4:4-5** – "But when the set time had fully come, God sent his Son, born of a woman, born under the law, to redeem those under the law, that we might receive adoption to sonship."

6. **Isaiah 9:6-7** – "For to us a child is born, to us a son is given, and the government will be on His shoulders. And He will be called Wonderful Counselor, Mighty God, Everlasting Father, Prince of Peace. Of the greatness of His government and peace there will be no end. He will reign on David's throne and over His kingdom, establishing and upholding it with justice and righteousness from that time on and forever. The zeal of the Lord Almighty will accomplish this."

7. **Luke 2:13-14** – "Suddenly a great company of the heavenly host appeared with the angel, praising God and saying, 'Glory to God in the highest heaven, and on earth peace to those on whom his favor rests.'"

8. **1 John 5:11** – "And this is the testimony: God has given us eternal life, and this life is in his Son."

9. **James 1:17-18** – "Every good and perfect gift is from above, coming down from the Father of the heavenly lights, who does not change like shifting shadows. He chose to give us birth through the Word of Truth, that we might be a kind of firstfruits of all he created."

10. **Romans 15:13** – "May the God of hope fill you with all joy and peace as you trust in Him, so that you may overflow with hope by the power of the Holy Spirit."

~Shepherd's Meal~
~TRADITION~

By: Tara Davis

Here's a fun, interactive way to give your children a taste of the excitement of Jesus' birth and His loving sacrifice for us: Begin a Shepherd's Meal tradition. Putting yourself in the place of the shepherds on the night Jesus was born adds another beautiful perspective to the Christmas story.

Materials:

- Bible
- A blanket
- Candles or flashlights
- A dark evening

Directions:

1. Prepare a simple meal; just use what you have on hand! Think of foods shepherds may have eaten in the time of Jesus—possibly just a simple stew (even a can from the grocery store) and bread. Use your imagination! The meal doesn't have to be perfect or accurate; your kids will remember how they felt more than the food they ate.

2. When the sun goes down, spread a blanket on your floor, light some candles, and serve your meal picnic-style.

3. As your kids are eating, grab a flashlight and your Bible and read the account of Jesus' birth in Luke 2, from the shepherds perspective. If you have young children, read the account from a children's Bible or storybook that's easy to understand.

4. Have your children imagine that they are shepherds out in the field enjoying dinner, when suddenly the sky fills with angels singing praise to Jesus.

Discussion:

- Ask how they would feel, and remind them how absolutely awe-inspiring an experience like this would be.
- Talk about how magnificent Jesus is and that He deserves our praise every day.
- Ask your children how they can bring glory to Jesus this Christmas season and throughout the year to come!

Bonus:

If your kids want to dress up like shepherds for your meal, you can make easy no-sew shepherd costumes in just minutes! Grab an old sheet or buy one from your local thrift store. Cut out a rectangle approximately 4x5 feet for a medium-sized child (You can always cut it down later if it ends up being too long). Fold this rectangle in half lengthwise and cut a half-circle the size of half a salad plate in the center of the fabric along the fold to make a neck hole. Place the fabric over the child's head. Cut a long thin strip of fabric for a belt, another 2x3 foot strip for a head covering, and a shorter thin strip to tie around your child's head to secure the head covering. This doesn't have to be perfect in any way. Older kids can even make their own costumes if they so desire. Remember, it is just for fun!

Christmas

~ Week Four ~

Precious Mama,

Are you feeling like you've failed before Christmas has even begun this year? Are you like me? Presents still unwrapped (even unpurchased), cookies unbaked, to-do lists unchecked? While feeling overwhelmed by the things I have not had time to accomplish this month, the Holy Spirit spoke His truth to my heart: "This season, this Holy-Day, is not about you or your Pinterest boards. It has never been about finishing the books or the crafts or the Advent Calendar. It's not about buying the perfect present for that person in your life. Those things do not matter when cast in the light of Jesus and His love. This time is about Him."

These next few days could become a mad rush to do more before Christmas Eve. Instead, let's bow our hearts in worship to our God. Humbly give Him your meager offerings that He can turn into miracles.

It may be too late to put together handmade gifts for my neighbors, but I do have all the time in the world to lift up my praise and thanksgiving to Jesus for the amazing gift of Himself.

Let go of those unmet expectations and allow Christ to bathe you in His grace in these next few days. Let Him wash away all of those expectations, stresses, and feelings of failure, and replace them with His perfect peace.

Transition your heart from a place of striving and stress to a place of worship. We do not need more cookies or fancy wrapped presents under the tree. We need more Jesus. We need His presence in our hearts and homes. That is what will make this Christmas truly beautiful.

May you relax and anticipate celebrating your perfect Savior. He is truly the only thing that matters this Christmas.

Much love to you! Merry Christmas!

Tara Davis and the Help Club for Moms Team

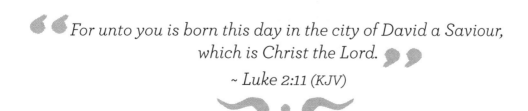

For unto you is born this day in the city of David a Saviour, which is Christ the Lord.

~ Luke 2:11 (KJV)

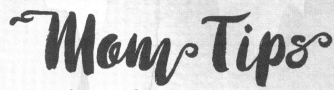

Mom Tips

By: Leslie Leonard

"For to us a child is born, to us a son is given, and the government will be on his shoulders. And he will be called Wonderful Counselor, Mighty God, Everlasting Father, Prince of Peace." ~ Isaiah 9:6

The Wise Woman Builds Her Spirit

- As we prepare our Christmas celebrations, commit to serving your loved ones with peace, love, kindness, and joy. Ask Jesus to SHINE His light through you while you are running errands, preparing meals, and tucking in little ones.
- Consider inviting someone over to celebrate Christmas with your family: a neighbor, college student, someone with family far away, or no family at all. We are all one family of God!

The Wise Woman Loves Her Husband

- Have a Christmas Eve Date Night with your husband. While the children are asleep, make some tea or hot cocoa, snuggle up on the couch with some cookies, and watch your favorite Christmas movie.
- Write a heartfelt Christmas card for your husband. Pray about what to write. Tell him how much you appreciate him, and point out how he has grown as a man of God. Mention the good plans God has for him, and be specific.

The Wise Woman Loves Her Children

- Read your children the Christmas story in Luke 2:1-20.
- Make gifts for neighbors. Even a dozen cookies on a paper plate is sweet! Walk to their door with your children and show them how to spread the love of Jesus at Christmas to those around you!

The Wise Woman Cares For Her Home

- Plan your meals for Christmas at the beginning of the week. Do any necessary grocery shopping and food prep to eliminate stress.
- Each day, set a timer for 20 minutes and clean your house with Christmas music playing. It is easier to enjoy your family and focus on Jesus when you are not distracted by clutter and mess.

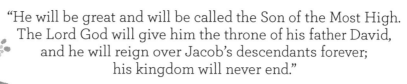

"He will be great and will be called the Son of the Most High.
The Lord God will give him the throne of his father David,
and he will reign over Jacob's descendants forever;
his kingdom will never end."

~ Luke 1:32-33

"Not only was Christ's miraculous birth prophetically revealed, but God planned his lineage from the very beginning."
~ Jesus Film Project

- Remember to call your prayer partner today. Pray over your Christmas celebrations, your guests, the work you have left to do, and whatever else comes to mind.

- This time of year, there is always something delicious to drink; pour some hot apple cider, cocoa, or coffee, and plan to exercise some spiritual muscles this morning!

- You will need your Bible for a lot of cross-referencing today. Get ready to turn some pages. We are about to unveil a mystery!

Prophecy of the Messiah

By: Rae-Ellen Sanders

Christmas is such an anticipated time of year! Children of all ages long for the festive lights, decorations, tasty treats, and Christmas carols that herald the days of giving and receiving gifts. However, the excitement that bubbles up within us cannot be compared to the anticipation the Jews had for the birth of the Messiah! Have you ever read the Christmas story and felt the enthusiasm the shepherds must have had as they rushed to Bethlehem to see Baby Jesus? The entire nation of Israel had longed for their Savior for centuries!

For years, the Jewish nation looked for the Messiah to lift them above the persecution and political unrest they had been living in. At the time of Jesus' birth, Rome had taken over Jerusalem and subverted their customs and religion, challenging them to change their ways. The Israelites longed for the prophecy to be fulfilled and for the promised Messiah to save them. I imagine they awaited with even more zeal and hope than we do for Christmas morning!

> But the angel said to them, "Do not be afraid. I bring you good news that will cause great joy for all the people. Today in the town of David a Savior has been born to you; he is the Messiah, the Lord. This will be a sign to you: You will find a baby wrapped in cloths and lying in a manger" (Luke 2:10-12).

For those who were educated at the time, they would have known the signs according to the prophets of old. It wasn't a mystery that the Messiah was coming as a baby, but they did not expect a humble birth; they expected him to be born in a palace with wealth and power. In fact, as the Magi were on their way to greet Jesus and bestow on him gifts, they stopped to search in Jerusalem, known as the City of the Great King (Matthew 5:35). After they provided King Herod with their strategy of searching for a sign and following the star, they keenly grasped Herod's ruthless plan to maintain his throne at any cost. God confirmed in a dream that they were not to return with the news of the child and to go home a different route (Hosea 11:1; Matthew 2:13-16).

The gift the world received was the very Son of God: a Prophet, Priest, and King who walked among them blameless and holy, born as an infant in the humblest of places. Isaiah 9:6-9 indicates that Jesus would not only be the Messiah, but also the Prince of Peace and King forever:

> For to us a child is born, to us a son is given, and the government will be on his shoulders. And he will be called Wonderful Counselor, Mighty God, Everlasting Father, Prince of Peace. Of the greatness of his government and peace there will be no end. He will reign on David's throne and over his kingdom, establishing and upholding it with justice and righteousness from that time on and forever. The zeal of the LORD Almighty will accomplish this.

Nothing is random with God; every detail is intentional and purposely orchestrated. He specifically gives us over 300 prophetic clues throughout Scripture about the Messiah. Clues about Jesus' birth and lineage are foretold all the way from Abraham, Ruth, King David, Elizabeth and Mary.

> Therefore the Lord himself will give you a sign: The virgin will conceive and give birth to a son, and will call him Immanuel. (Isaiah 7:14)

> All this took place to fulfill what the Lord had said through the prophet: "The virgin will conceive and give birth to a son, and they will call him Immanuel" (which means God with us). (Matthew 1:22-23)

God knew we needed a Savior and planned in advance to send his very own Son. John 3:16 says, "For God so loved the world that he gave his one and only Son, that whoever believes in him shall not perish but have eternal life." As Christmas approaches, allow God's prophetic words and master plan to sink into the depths of your heart. Ponder the indescribable gift of Jesus' miraculous birth: the heavens opening up, the angels proclaiming the GOOD NEWS, and the lowly manger scene that represents how Jesus came for ALL mankind to see the extent of God's love. Reflect with new anticipation the free gift of eternal life and the life-altering rewards we receive by faith in the finished work of Jesus Christ. Invite Immanuel (God with us) to dwell afresh in your heart, and to be illuminated in your Christmas activities this year!

Questions to Ponder:

- When God makes a promise in His Word, He asks us to believe. Do you really believe the Word of God? Many Jews are still waiting for the Messiah to come for the first time because they haven't accepted Jesus as the Messiah. Others, called Messianic Jews, faithfully believe Jesus came to fulfill the Law. How do you respond to the claim of Jesus the Messiah being God himself? Ask the God of Abraham, Isaac, and Jacob if Jesus/Yeshua is the Messiah. He will lead you in all truth!

Faith-Filled Ideas:

Often, you will see passages repeated throughout Scripture to demonstrate the prophecy being fulfilled thousands of years later. Have you ever found New Testament passages that confirm Old Testament prophecy? There are over 48 Messianic prophecies and 324 individual prophecies in God's Word. If this wows you, there are other resources to help you do an exhaustive search. **Challenge yourself to read these Scriptures this season and be in awe of our infinite, omnipotent, everlasting Father!**

Matthew 1:1-17
Romans 9:4-5

2 Samuel 7:12-17
Romans 1:2-4

Micah 5:2
Matthew 2:4-6

Isaiah 42:1-7
Matthew 12:15-21

Isaiah 61:1-3
Luke 4:16-19

Malachi 3:1
Isaiah 40:3-5
Matthew 3:1-3
Matthew 3:16-17
Luke 3:3-6
John 1:23

Zechariah 9:9
Matthew 21:1-11

1 Samuel 2:35
Hebrews 2:17

Jeremiah 23:5
Psalm 110:1
Matthew 22:44
Mark 12:36
Luke 20:42

Psalm 17:7
Psalm 18:35
Psalm 20:6
Psalm 73:23

Matthew 26:64
Mark 14:62
Mark 16:19
Luke 22:69

Acts 2:25
Acts 5:31
Acts 7:55-56
Romans 8:34
Hebrews 8:1

journal

"When they saw the star, they were overjoyed."

~ Matthew 2:10

"Those who are wise will shine like the brightness of the heavens, and those who lead many to righteousness, like the stars for ever and ever."

~ Daniel 12:3

- Oh, how our Savior is waiting to meet with you! Go to your comfortable spot and bring along your Bible, journal, and pen. Don't forget your favorite drink. For me, it is a coffee with two creams and three sugars. Our Lord has amazing things for us today!

- Please read Matthew 2:1-12. Write verse 10 in your journal. Sit quietly and ponder this verse. If any word stands out, circle or underline it in your journal. Don't rush this process. Let time stand still as God speaks to you.

The Star of Bethlehem

By: Susan Proctor

A few days ago, I heard a new Christmas song from Sidewalk Prophets called, 'Hey Moon.' It tells the Christmas story from the perspective of the Star of Bethlehem, and how it had a major role in the Christmas story to point the Magi or Wisemen to Jesus. The Star is a bright thread in the tapestry of Jesus' life, yet as I began to ponder the purpose of the star, my heart was encouraged and convicted. It had two very profound purposes: leading the Wisemen to Jesus and bringing hope to a dry and desolate land.

There are trillions of stars, each one just a point of light in the sky, until Jesus entered into the picture. We, too, are like the Star of Bethlehem. We were created for the purpose of bringing glory to God. Radiating the joy of our salvation reveals our gracious, loving Savior to those around us. Sharing a smile, saying a genuine "hello," offering words of encouragement, or leading someone in a prayer of salvation, are a few ways to make a difference in the world.

We can spotlight Jesus just like the star did by being kind and loving to those around us.

Philippians 2:14-15 (CSB) tells us,

> Do everything without grumbling and arguing, so that you may be blameless and pure, children of God who are faultless in a crooked and perverted generation, among whom you shine like stars in the world.

Sometimes, the hardest people to love are the ones who need it the most. Recently, I was having a tough day at the grocery store, feeling grouchy and irritable, when a sweet older lady stopped to compliment me for doing a great job with my three youngest children. Her sweet encouragement gave me the energy to finish shopping with joy!

Hope makes an enormous difference, and our world is looking for hope, which may be why Christmas sales, decorations, and music make an earlier appearance every year. Most stores start getting Christmas decorations out at the end of summer! It is amazing how fast it comes! Even the cynical are transported into an enchanted fantasy by the twinkling lights, beautifully bedecked trees, and pretty packages of wishes fulfilled. Hope comes flooding over them.

Though this wonderland is lovely, the true magic of Christmas is in the transformation of people because of the birth of Jesus: Strangers become friends, chaos turns to peace, and stress becomes laughter and joy. It is a season in which the unexpected and most wanted happens.

God has made us to "shine like stars" in this dark and crooked world. Don't let grumbling or arguing steal your joy and dim your light. Matthew 5:16 instructs, "...let your light shine before men, that they may see your good deeds and glorify your Father in heaven." The stark contrast of being blameless, pure, and full of good deeds to worldly grumbling, arguing, and self-gratification is a source of hope, and leads those around us to give glory to our Father in Heaven. Jesus cannot be hidden when we truly allow Him to shine through us just like the Star of Bethlehem.

Questions to Ponder:

• Are you shining like a star or are you full of complaining and bitterness? If you are struggling to see the positives, lay down the negatives at Jesus' feet. Recently, I was struggling to see the good things of God. So, I wrote in my journal all the negative things. Afterward, I prayed and left them at the feet of God. Soon next to each of those complaints, God provided. Sometimes, it was a rebuke with Scripture. Other times, He fixed the problem or made me see things from a different perspective. The bottom line was that I no longer saw all the negatives, just His provision.

• How can you shine Jesus to others around you?

Faith-Filled Ideas:

(Pick one that will work for you)

Wherever you go—library, grocery store, karate, dance, mall, church—greet people with a smile and say, "Merry Christmas!" I have yet to get a hateful look or a rude remark. Most of the time, people are astonished that I care enough to speak.

As you are going about life, find someone to encourage. It could be a young mom, an older person, a small child, your husband, or your mother-in-law. I pray often that God would allow someone to come across my path into whom I can speak life.

When you go to restaurants, ask your waiter/waitress how you can pray for him/her. It may feel awkward at first, but they will be so appreciative. I have even had one waitress stop and pray with us. Don't forget to tip well because you are Jesus' shining star!

journal

_____

_____

_____

journal

_____

_____

_____

_____

_____

_____

_____

_____

_____

_____

_____

_____

_____

_____

_____

_____

_____

_____

_____

_____

_____

_____

_____

_____

_____

_____

_____

_____

_____

Christmas ~ Week Four

"On coming to the house, they saw the child with his mother Mary, and they bowed down and worshiped him. Then they opened their treasures and presented him with gifts of gold, frankincense and myrrh."

~ Matthew 2:11

"God rewards those who seek Him. Not those who seek doctrine of religion or systems or creeds. Many settle for these lesser passions, but the reward goes to those who settle for nothing less than Jesus himself. And what is the reward? What awaits those who seek Jesus? Nothing short of the heart of Jesus."
~ Max Lucado

- How is your heart today? Ask God that He would reveal Himself to you through the study of His Word.
- Grab your Bible, find a comfortable spot in front of your Christmas tree, and let's look at what it means to seek the Lord in Matthew 2:1-12. Go ahead and write verse 11 in your journal.

Wise Women Seek Jesus

By: Tara Davis

Sweet mamas, you have worked so hard these past weeks making Christmas special for your family. The rush of this season can be exhausting! When I am busy, my eyes tend to focus anywhere but on Jesus. However during this crazy, sweet season, God is calling us to seek His grace, to worship Him, and to find ourselves at peace in His arms.

How do we actively seek that baby, Word became flesh, the embodiment of all Truth, born two thousand years ago? How can we possibly scrape together enough energy for worship after we have spent it all on this long journey toward Christmas Day?

The Wisemen in Matthew were some of the most unlikely people to seek the baby Jesus. They were Gentiles from a country far away who came to worship the long-prophesied "King of the Jews." Moreover, they had to travel up to two years to find Jesus, guided simply by a star and their knowledge of ancient Scripture.

What a long, challenging journey! However, they persisted in their resolution to see the Savior of the World. Each time they saw the star appear to guide them, they were recipients of God's grace.

Do you feel as if you are on a long, exhausting journey this Christmas? Possibly a journey leading you further from the Lord, as opposed to closer to His heart? Look up! God is shining His light of grace on you just as He did for the Wisemen! He tells us in 2 Peter 1:19 that there is a Day-Star arising in the hearts of those that seek Christ! Jesus is just waiting to shine His glorious, healing light into every corner of your life!

He will be your strength as you seek His Son this season. He promises in Jeremiah 29:13, "You will seek me and find me, when you seek me with all your heart." Trust Him with your heart and your desire for Him. He has many great things to show you! In love, He whispers, "Call to me and I will answer you and tell you great and unsearchable things you do not know" (Jeremiah 33:3).

When the Wisemen finally found Jesus, the purpose of their seeking was fulfilled as they fell down and worshiped Him. When you find the Savior this Christmas and beyond, in all of the busyness and mess of life, humble yourself in worship.

"I urge you therefore...to present your bodies a living and holy sacrifice, acceptable to God, which is your spiritual service of worship" (Romans 12:1 NASB). Present your strengths, weaknesses, desires, talents, and failings to Him to use as He wishes. Giving Him the very things that you hold closest to your heart is the ultimate act of adoration.

As this Christmas season ends and a new year begins, would you join me in seeking Jesus, asking Him to reveal Himself in a way only He is able? Commit to surrendering yourself, resting in His goodness and love. He wants you to seek Him and find Him, sweet friend! Enjoy His presence and the gift of His grace in the days to come.

Questions to Ponder:

- Has it been hard for you to keep your focus on Christ this Christmas season?

- How can you commit to seeking Him as Christmas comes to a close and a new year opens wide before you?

Faith-Filled Ideas:

In worship, the Wisemen presented Jesus with very precious gifts. What can you give to your Savior today? On a small piece of paper, have each of your family members write down a gift they will give to the Lord this Christmas. Give from a heart of sacrifice as opposed to places of excess in your life. What do you need to turn over to the Lord? With what do you need to trust Him? Keep these papers in a small decorative box or in a stocking, and bring them out next Christmas to read over with new commitment.

Journal

_____

_____

_____

_____

_____

_____

_____

_____

_____

_____

The first hint of snow makes me think of peppermint and chocolate, in my coffee but also in my dessert. Growing up in New Jersey means that I know good New York style cheesecake! I mention that because there are plenty of peppermint confections out there that add candy cane bits to the actual cheesecake filling. This makes the cheesecake crunchy and sticky. My opinion is that you shouldn't mess up the authentic consistency of rich cheesecake. This Candy Cane Cheesecake has just the right balance of creamy cheesecake filling with the added flavor of peppermint extract, a delicious explosion of peppermint flavored Oreo crust, and a shiny dark chocolate ganache that drips down the sides. The "top chocolate layer" becomes an ice skating rink of ganache—your wonderland for candy cane decoration. If you love cheesecake, peppermint, and Oreos, you'll love this dessert! Put on some Christmas music and hum along as you create this masterpiece.

CANDY CANE CHEESECAKE By: Rae-Ellen Sanders

Ingredients:

Oreo crust:

24 Peppermint Bark-flavored Oreos or Trader Joe's Candy Cane Joe Joe's

5 Tbsp of melted butter

Cheesecake Filling:

32 oz (4 bars) full-fat cream cheese bricks

4 eggs

¾ cup sour cream

½ cups sugar

¼ tsp of salt

3 Tbsp of flour

2 tsp of vanilla extract

2 tsp of peppermint extract

Dark Chocolate Ganache:

10 oz of Ghirardelli dark chocolate chips

1 cup heavy whipping cream

Directions:

1. Line the bottom of a 9-inch springform pan with parchment paper and grease/spray the sides of the pan. Wrap a piece of heavy-duty foil securely around the bottom of the springform pan to make sure no water gets in during the baking. Place springform pan on top of a roasting pan and wait to add water just before baking. (This process is called a water bath.)

2. Preheat the oven to 350 degrees.

Food for the Soul

CANDY CANE CHEESECAKE

By: Rae-Ellen Sanders

Oreo Crust Directions:

1. Use the old-fashioned method of rolling a rolling pin over a baggy of cookies, or utilize a chopper to crush cookies into crumbs.
2. Melt butter and then fold in crumbs.
3. Press into bottom of springform pan evenly.
4. Set in the fridge or freezer to firm the crust while making the filling.

Cheesecake Filling:

1. In a large bowl, beat cream cheese and sugar until smooth.
2. Add eggs one at a time.
3. Mix in the sour cream, flour, salt, and extracts. Beat on low speed until just combined. Don't over mix as this can cause cracking in the surface of the cake.

Directions:

1. Pour cheesecake filling over the Oreo crust. Smooth the top.
2. Add HOT water to the roasting pan, up to half the side of the springform pan.
3. Reduce the oven temperature to 325 degrees and bake for 1 hour and 45 minutes. The center should be a tiny bit jiggly. Turn OFF the oven, open the door, and leave the cheesecake in the oven for an additional 30 minutes.
4. Remove the springform pan from the water bath, dry the bottom, and cool it on a wire rack for 10 minutes. Carefully run a knife around the edge of the pan to loosen. DON'T release the springform just yet! Cover and refrigerate for at least 4 hours or overnight.
5. Remove cheesecake from refrigerator to unhinge the sides and remove springform collar. Transfer the cake to your serving platter.
6. Make ganache by heating the heavy whipping cream and chocolate chips in the microwave for 30 seconds or until warm. Whisk gently until the chocolate melts and the mixture develops a smooth, shiny texture. Pour the ganache over the cheesecake, allowing it to run in ripples down the sides. Place cake back into the fridge to harden the ganache.
7. Decorate with peppermint candy of your choice. Try using different sizes and shapes, like crushed peppermint candy, shards of peppermint bark, lollipops, candy canes, round peppermints, and ribbon candy.
8. Use a sharp knife to cut into the hardened ganache and enjoy this new Christmas favorite!

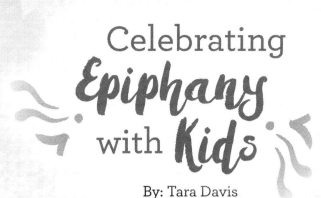

Celebrating Epiphany with Kids

By: Tara Davis

Every year as I clean up our Christmas and begin putting decor and toys away, I feel a twinge of regret. No matter how strong we start December with Advent activities, special Christmas books, and traditions that encourage my children to focus their eyes on Jesus and the true meaning of Christmas, we always finish in a messy, exhausted heap.

I want things to be different. I want to wrap up Christmas with a heart of worship. I want my children to begin the new year with hearts filled to the brim with the love of our Savior, instead of frazzled from the hustle and bustle of the holidays. Maybe you feel the same, my friend? This year, I may have found at least part of the answer: celebrating Epiphany Day with my kids!

Historically, Epiphany is celebrated on January 6th and wraps up the Twelve Days of Christmas, which begin on December 25th. This beautiful, Christ-centered celebration provides a wonderful opportunity to teach our children that Jesus came as a Savior King for all who choose to believe!

Why don't you celebrate Epiphany with us this year? It may become a fun new tradition for your children as it has for mine! The message of Epiphany focuses on the three Wisemen, gentiles from the East who traveled a great distance just to have the chance to worship the prophesied King. I love that they traveled all that way to simply worship Him! I love that, even though they were not of Jewish descent, they knew Jesus was their King, the KING of ALL kings.

In my family, we celebrate Epiphany by making a simple cake, creating Wisemen crowns, singing songs of worship, and reading the account of the Wisemen in Matthew 2:1-12. We also unwrap a box filled with gold, frankincense, and myrrh (instructions below) and talk about the meaning of each of these gifts and how they each foretold a bit of what was to come in the life of Jesus. We finish by discussing what it means for us to seek Jesus each day of the new year and how we can live a life of worship before Him. Mama, this is such a sweet tradition to add to your Christmas season! Try it this year!

Easy Wisemen Crowns:

Cut a rectangular shape out of construction or computer paper long enough to wrap completely around your child's head. You will probably need to staple two sheets of paper together and cut a bit off the end to make it the right length. Next, cut the top edge in a large zig-zag; this will be the points of the crown. Let your child decorate with markers or crayons and finish by wrapping the crown around the child's head to fit and stapling the ends together. You can even make a miniature version of this crown do decorate your Epiphany cake!

Christmas Songs of Worship:

"Joy to the World," "Silent Night," and "Hark the Herald Angels Sing."

Celebrating
Epiphany
with *Kids*

By: Tara Davis

Box of Gold, Frankincense, and Myrrh Instructions:

- **Gold**, represented by a gold-painted rock, symbolizes royalty. By bringing a gift of gold, the Wisemen acknowledged that Jesus truly is the King of Kings.

- **Frankincense**, represented by dried sap from a pine tree or a little bottle of perfume or oil. Frankincense is actually an aromatic gum resin that is still widely used in parts of the Middle East and Africa today. Frankincense was used in the temple as a pure offering to the Lord. A parallel can be drawn between this and Jesus' life as a pure and holy offering to the Lord.

- **Myrrh**, represented by fake white flowers or flowers cut from paper, was an anointing oil. Perhaps the Wisemen intended this gift as an indication of Jesus' humanity and the manner in which he would save his people—namely, that he would die for them and his body would be anointed with myrrh at His burial.

Discussion:

Talk to your kids about how we as believers can start life anew this year by daily acknowledging Jesus as our King! How would that look practically in their lives? Would they treat others differently? How would their thoughts change toward Jesus? Would they bow their hearts in reverence before Him?

New Year's

My Dear Friends,

We at the Help Club for Moms pray your Christmas was infused with the presence of the Lord in every moment of your celebration.

But what do we do now? All the packages have been opened and the day we have awaited with great anticipation and preparation has passed.

Remember that Emmanuel has come! God is with us! He is here to walk with you through every day of your life. As we look ahead to the New Year, it's time to set aside regrets from the past and anticipate what God has for you in the coming year.

Isaiah 43:18-19a says, "Forget the former things; do not dwell on the past. See, I am doing a new thing! Now it springs up; do you not perceive it?"

What is the one thing you are going to do differently in the New Year that will help you make every day a celebration of Christmas?

For me, that one thing will be spending more time with my Savior—more time sitting at the feet of Jesus: The lover of my soul. Can we ever get enough time with Him?

The only way we can truly spend enough time with Him is when we live a lifestyle of ceaseless prayer. The emptiness in our hearts will be filled, not by spending just the first moments of our days with Him, but by inviting Him into each and every moment.

We pray that God will speak to you through the Bible studies this week to transform you "into his likeness with ever-increasing glory, which comes from the Lord, who is the Spirit" (2 Corinthians 3:18).

With love,

Jennifer Valdois and the Help Club For Moms Team

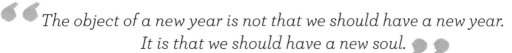

The object of a new year is not that we should have a new year. It is that we should have a new soul.
~ G. K. Chesterton

Mom Tips

By: Leslie Leonard

"Forget the former things; do not dwell on the past."
~ Isaiah 43:18

The Wise Woman Builds Her Spirit

- Ask God for a Bible verse for next year. Write your verse down in a prominent place in your home and memorize it. Don't be discouraged if a verse is not readily brought to mind. Keep praying, the Lord will reveal one to you.
- Create a plan to read God's Word next year. There are several plans to read the Bible in a year. Audio Bibles are great too! The *Daily Audio Bible* is fantastic!

The Wise Woman Loves Her Husband

- Give your husband a free night this week. Encourage him to connect with a friend face-to-face.
- Create a list of requests to pray for your husband for next year. Be specific about needs and areas of growth you will commit to the Lord in prayer. Put your list in your prayer binder for reference.

The Wise Woman Loves Her Children

- Take your children for a winter nature walk. Make a list of 10 items you hope to find, grab your coats, and head outside.
- Create a list of requests to pray for each of your children for next year. Be specific about needs and areas of growth to commit to the Lord in prayer. Put your list in your prayer binder for reference.

The Wise Woman Cares For Her Home

- Take time to write thank-you notes. Use the last 10 minutes of your quiet time to write one or two a day until you are finished.
- Mark on your calendar the day you will take down your Christmas decorations. When packing up the boxes, use brightly colored duct tape to label and number them. Include on your label the total number of boxes in your Christmas collection. (If you have 3 boxes, your labels will read: 1 of 3, 2 of 3, and 3 of 3.) Write a summary list of the contents of each container and put it in or on the box, or in a file. Not only will this help you find specific decorations, it will help you re-pack each box.

> "'Who can hide in secret places so that I cannot see him?'
> declares the Lord. 'Do not I fill heaven and earth?'
> declares the Lord."
>
> ~ Jeremiah 23:24

"There is not in the world a kind of life more sweet and delightful, than that of a continual conversation with God; those only can comprehend it who practice and experience it."
~ Brother Lawrence

- It's Monday and time to pray with your prayer partner! If you don't have someone as a designated prayer partner, call a friend right now and pray with her for 10 minutes. Take turns praying for each other. Remember that you are moving heaven as you pray!

- It's time to meet with your beloved Jesus! Grab your Bible, a pen, a journal, something hot to drink, and a beautiful-smelling candle. Take a deep breath. Calm your heart and mind. Focus your thoughts on the truth that Jesus loves you and longs for you to know how close He is with you; in fact, He is closer than your breath. Pray right now for God to speak to your heart through today's Bible study about becoming more aware of His presence and increasing your faith in knowing He is with you. Be here with Jesus, right now at this moment.

- Read Psalm 131:1-3, Jeremiah 23:24, and 1 Corinthians 3:16. Write Psalm 131:2 in your journal.

How to Practice God's Presence

By: Deb Weakly

Some time ago, while sitting in the choir loft of a beautiful church waiting for the choir director to start practice, I had a thousand thoughts swirling around in my head. I was too busy to sing and felt overwhelmed at the thought of all I had on my plate that week that still needed to be done. It always seems as if I never have enough time to finish what I need to do.

It was then that I felt the Lord impress upon me the thought, "Be here with me, Deb. Be here." God wanted me to be with Him at that moment and to let everything else go. I simply prayed a quick prayer asking God to show me how to become more aware of His presence and to be with Him right at that moment. Instantly, I felt my body relax, and I began to look around at the scene in the choir loft. I noticed the director's wonderful sense of humor, the other choir members' sweet love for Jesus, and the beauty of the music we were singing. I observed the magnificent stained glass window and said to God, "Oh, what a beautiful window! I know when they were building this church, they prayed for wisdom, and look how You answered!! It's gorgeous!"

Since then, I find myself pondering and praying about how to be aware of the presence of God. In Jeremiah 23:24, Scripture says that God is around us at all times, and according to 1 Corinthians 3:16, the Spirit of God dwells in all believers. So if you are a Christ follower, He lives in you!

But why don't we always feel God? How can we become more aware of Him? Sometimes we feel alone, but God's Word says that His Spirit lives in us. There can be many factors as to why we don't feel God, but one way we can begin to learn to become aware of Him is to practice His presence. Just like everything else in life, when we practice something, we become better and better at it. But how do you practice being aware of God's presence?

- **Start by spending regular time with God.** The "Morning Watch" is a wonderful term used to describe the first few moments of the day spent with God. Of course, you can talk to God any time, but there is something special about meeting with Him in prayer and Bible reading first thing in the morning. The more time you spend with God, the better you will know His Word, and the easier it will be to hear His voice. You will learn to hear Him when He is teaching you or encouraging you, and also when He is convicting you of sin or warning you that you are headed in the wrong direction. When you spend time with God, you will learn to hear His voice in such a way that makes it easier to be in closer fellowship with Him. If mornings are tough for you, ask God to wake you up 15 minutes earlier and help you to focus on Him right away. Trust me He will honor this request!

- **Next, ask God to help you to cultivate a mental habit of noticing His presence.** Ask Him several times a day to help you feel His peace and start to notice the beauty around you–like the smallness of your children's fingers, the love in your husband's eyes when he looks at you, the delicious smell of bread baking in the oven, or the sweet sound of worship music playing in the background. For a few minutes, be gratefully present in each moment with God, conversing with Him about each of the gifts you observe.

- **Lastly, the Bible says that worship and a thankful heart ushers us into God's presence.** Psalm 22:3 says, "God inhabits the praise of His people." God loves it when we notice His blessings. A thankful heart leads us to worship, which brings joy to our hearts and also an increased awareness of His love and nearness.

Remember, whether you feel happy or sad, or your circumstances are good or bad, God is always with you. There is never a moment when you are without God's presence (Hebrews 13:5).

"Think often on God, by day, by night, in your business and even in your diversions. He is always near you and with you; leave him not alone." ~ Brother Lawrence

Questions to Ponder:

- When have you felt God's presence the most? Were you worshipping at church, rocking your baby to sleep, or enduring a difficult trial? If you can't pinpoint a moment, ask God to remind you as a touchstone to encourage you when He seems distant.

Faith-Filled Ideas:

Write "Practice God's Presence" on your bathroom mirror with a dry erase marker to daily spur you on to practice the ideas in this study. Go through the steps outlined over and over until they are committed to your memory.

Record today's verses on your phone's recording device. Listen to them often to remind yourself of the truth that God is with you. Ask Him to help you to rest in His presence like the weaned child with its mother in Psalm 131:2.

journal

_____
_____
_____
_____
_____
_____
_____
_____
_____
_____
_____
_____
_____
_____
_____
_____
_____
_____
_____
_____
_____
_____
_____
_____
_____
_____
_____

"She will give birth to a son,
and you are to give him the name Jesus,
because he will save his people from their sins."

~ Matthew 1:21

"There is power in the name of Jesus to break every chain."
~ from the song "Break Every Chain" By: Will Regan, United Pursuit

- Feeling fatigued? Open up your Bible and notebook. Before you sit down, do 10 jumping jacks. You've pumped your heart, now pump your soul!
- Read Matthew 1:18-25. Write verse 21 in your journal. Highlight the word "save." Make it stand out with asterisks, stars, or fireworks. It's an important word!

The Name of Jesus

By: Daphne Close

Christmas season has officially ended. Reflections on "The Best of the Year" have begun. The radio has replaced around-the-clock Christmas music with the annual countdown of the year's most popular songs. Which song will be #1 on the chart? Christmas trees litter our curbsides; holiday decorations now cost less than half of their original price. You may be trying to decide whether to go out for New Year's Eve or to just stay home. How can we keep the message of Christmas in our hearts as we prepare for the new year? Let's go back to the beginning of the Christmas story to find inspiration for the new year. Today, we will reflect on Jesus' father, Joseph.

> This is how the birth of Jesus the Messiah came about: His mother Mary was pledged to be married to Joseph, but before they came together, she was found to be pregnant through the Holy Spirit. Because Joseph her husband was faithful to the law, and yet did not want to expose her to public disgrace, he had in mind to divorce her quietly. But after he had considered this, an angel of the Lord appeared to him in a dream and said, "Joseph son of David, do not be afraid to take Mary home as your wife, because what is conceived in her is from the Holy Spirit." (Matthew 1:18-20)

As I read this historical account from Joseph's perspective, I am curious as to what he was thinking. He was put in a very difficult situation, not of his own making. In fact, he was an upright, godly man being asked to husband a pregnant woman carrying a child he knew wasn't his. By faith, he trusted the Lord's messenger and married his betrothed. I wonder if, at some point, Joseph said to himself, "This is not how I expected my life to turn out." Why did God turn Joseph's life upside down?

> She will give birth to a son, and you are to give him the name Jesus, because he will save his people from their sins. (Matthew 1:21)

The name of Jesus means "He saves." I love the name of Jesus. It brings freedom! Romans 10:13 says, "Everyone who calls on the name of the Lord will be saved." His name brings ultimate, eternal deliverance from the wrath of God. I am certain that Joseph was grateful to be used of God in this way.

Many years ago, I was at a corporate worship night. It was one of those memories I'll never forget. Everyone was in awe of God, our hearts stirred to worship as we sang praise. The presence of the Lord was so strong. I remember being so full of joy, so full of passion, so full of love for the Lord, that I freely shouted at the top of my lungs, "Jesus!" Nothing more needed to be said. His name alone proclaimed the core of my worship.

There have been other times when I just didn't know what to say when my heart was overwhelmed with sorrow or I couldn't put words to my emotions. The only word that could come out was "Jesus." Just saying His name out loud brought great comfort.

Have you experienced or heard of Christians being spiritually oppressed? My friends described it as a great heaviness that weighed them down. They tried to pray, but the burden was too strong. Finally, with all they had within them, they cried out, "Jesus!" With this one word prayer, the burden lifted! The name of the Lord is so powerful that the enemy must leave.

Unfortunately for Israel, they rejected their Messiah, blind to the power of this beautiful name:

> In the same way the chief priests also, along with the scribes and elders, were mocking Him and saying, "He saved others; He cannot save Himself. He is the King of Israel; let Him now come down from the cross, and we will believe in Him." (Matthew 27:41-42 NASB)

Do you see the heartbreaking irony? They mocked Jesus, insulting His claims to save them. They rejected salvation from the very one whose name and human incarnation means, "He Saves."

From what situation, false belief, or unexpected life change do you want Jesus to save you? Let God's angel say to you, just as he said to Joseph, "Do not be afraid" (Matthew 1:20)!

Questions to Ponder:
- Do you feel lost in any way? In what area do you long to be saved? You can use the term "lost" and "saved" loosely. It could be that you feel lost in your daily to-do list, or you feel you don't belong at church, thus feeling lost. Perhaps you want to be saved from a medical condition. Whatever the context, ask Jesus to save you.

Faith-Filled Ideas:
Do you like to make New Year's resolutions? This year, resolve to see how Jesus will save you in one area. Remember, you cannot save yourself. Only Jesus can save. So pray, wait, listen, watch, and then marvel. Pray to the Lord, asking Him to take care of this area. Wait for His timing. Listen to God. Read His Word. Watch to see how His answer is greater than your plan. Finally, marvel at how He saved you.

Spend exactly one minute praising Jesus out loud, declaring the "I Am" names of Jesus listed below. For every name, say "Jesus, You are _____ ." Speak slowly and methodically, as if chewing on every word.

Further Study:
> For a child will be born to us, a son will be given to us; and the government will rest on His shoulders; and His name will be called Wonderful Counselor, Mighty God, Eternal Father, Prince of Peace. (Isaiah 9:6)

The 7 "I Am's" in John:

1. The Way
2. The Truth
3. The Life
4. The Light of the World
5. The Bread of Life
6. The Vine
7. The Gate
8. The Resurrection and Life
9. The Good Shepherd

Bible Resources provides a comprehensive list: www.bibleresources.org/names-of-jesus.

After you have practiced this form of worship on your own, try this with others. If your children can read, have them join you.

Journal

_____

_____

_____

_____

_____

_____

_____

_____

_____

_____

_____

_____

_____

_____

_____

_____

_____

_____

_____

_____

_____

"Forget the former things; do not dwell on the past.
See, I am doing a new thing! Now it springs up;
do you not perceive it? I am making a way
in the desert and streams in the wasteland."

~ Isaiah 43:18-19

"Let go of the old so you can completely take hold of the new."
~ Joyce Meyer

- Find a cozy place to spend time with your Lord today. Bring your Bible and your journal. Take a deep breath, calm your spirit, and notice the blessings around you. Rest in God's peace.
- Read Isaiah 43:16-21. Write Isaiah 43:18-19 in your journal.

Take Hold of God's Blessings

By: Heather Doolittle

New Year's resolutions speak to our innate desire to begin anew and transform into a better version of ourselves. The idea that each year brings a fresh start and new opportunities to learn and grow is not only appealing, it is Biblical. In fact, on Mount Sinai God commanded His people to spend the first 10 days of each New Year focusing on how to change and grow in the months ahead (Leviticus 23:23-28).

These 10 days are called the High Holy Days, culminating with the Day of Atonement on day 10. God's people observe them in earnest prayer, fasting, and introspection, as well as making amends (atoning) for transgressing God's Law before the Day of Atonement, starting each year with a clean slate to enjoy the blessings ahead. The High Holy Days are a beautiful celebration of God's grace and redemption.

Your sins don't accumulate throughout the year until the Day of Atonement arrives; God's mercies are new every morning (Lamentations 3:22-23). Hence, the Day of Atonement is for man, not for God. Even though He has readily forgiven all our sins, we don't always forgive ourselves so freely. Do you have burdens you have carried for years? Do you have a negative self-image or shame, or some unbearable sin you can't seem to get past? What about "mom guilt" from holding yourself to impossible standards?

Jesus has saved us from the bondage, penalty, and guilt of our sin. He has forgiven our sins, but we will only experience freedom when we receive that forgiveness (Galatians 5:1). Through this extended New Years celebration, we have an annual opportunity to shed our past mistakes and partake in the blessings our Father has laid before us. "Forget the former things; do not dwell on the past. See, I am doing a new thing!" (Isaiah 43:18). God made this promise when the Israelites were in the depths of despair, floundering in the dire consequences of their sin. Even in His discipline, God's mercy is glorious. To deeply enjoy life in Christ, we must stop dwelling in the past and live in the present in order to set our sights on a brighter future.

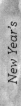

Just imagine what a difference it would make if you were to start this tradition. Each year, spend 10 days focusing on how God is moving in your life, just as God commanded the Israelites to do. Instead of beating yourself up over eating too many cookies or overspending over Christmas, just let the extraneous burdens go. Instead, focus on how God is working in your life and your heart. It is far too easy to miss what God is doing when you are focused on your own agenda. Chances are, the plans God has for you are better than anything you could come up with anyway!

Questions to Ponder:

• What thoughts, attitudes, or burdens are drawing your heart away from Jesus?

• In Jeremiah 33:3, God says, "Call to me and I will answer and tell you great and unsearchable things you do not know." Call to your Savior. Pray that He will show you how to let your burdens go, and trust that He will answer you. Lay your troubles at the cross, and leave them there.

Faith-Filled Ideas:

You may be able to come up with some worthy goals: organize your schedule, lose a few pounds, keep your house cleaner. These all may be good plans, but are they the best God has for you? Only God knows what is in store for the year ahead, so shouldn't you first consult Him before making your plans? Don't miss God while pursuing your agenda.

Over the next 10 days, use your quiet moments to draw near to God. Examine your life and your thoughts. Repent and let go of all guilt and condemnation. Talk to your Heavenly Father about how you can live better next year. Ask how He is working in your life, and how you can work with Him.

Journal

_____

_____

_____

_____

_____

_____

_____

_____

_____

_____

_____

_____

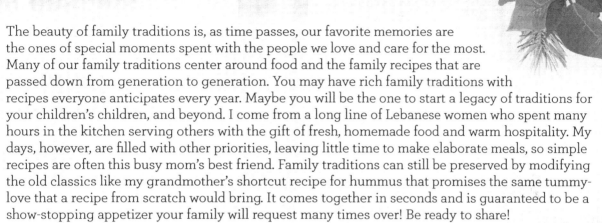

Food for the Soul

The beauty of family traditions is, as time passes, our favorite memories are the ones of special moments spent with the people we love and care for the most. Many of our family traditions center around food and the family recipes that are passed down from generation to generation. You may have rich family traditions with recipes everyone anticipates every year. Maybe you will be the one to start a legacy of traditions for your children's children, and beyond. I come from a long line of Lebanese women who spent many hours in the kitchen serving others with the gift of fresh, homemade food and warm hospitality. My days, however, are filled with other priorities, leaving little time to make elaborate meals, so simple recipes are often this busy mom's best friend. Family traditions can still be preserved by modifying the old classics like my grandmother's shortcut recipe for hummus that promises the same tummy-love that a recipe from scratch would bring. It comes together in seconds and is guaranteed to be a show-stopping appetizer your family will request many times over! Be ready to share!

YA-YA'S HUMMUS   By: Tonya Baldessari

Ingredients

2 lbs Sabra Roasted Red Pepper Hummus

⅓ cup bell peppers, chopped (red and green at Christmas time; otherwise, use yellow, red, and orange)

¼ cup cucumbers, chopped

2-3 Tbsp Feta cheese, crumbled

Olive oil to drizzle

Directions:

1. Choose a pretty platter or dish.
2. Spread the whole container of hummus onto the platter in an even layer.
3. Sprinkle the bell peppers, cucumbers, and Feta cheese evenly over the hummus.
4. Finish with olive oil generously drizzled over the entire platter.
5. Serve with Triscuits, veggies, pita chips, or anything else that's good for dipping.
6. (Triscuit Fire Roasted Tomato and Olive Oil & Garden Herb are my family's favorite cracker for enjoying Ya-Ya's Hummus!)

A Special
New Year's Eve
for Kids
By: Tara Davis

New Year's Eve is the perfect time to celebrate the blessings of the past year and look forward with excitement and anticipation to the coming days. Do you need some inspiration for fun activities for your family this New Year's Eve? Try some of these ideas!

MAKE A FAMILY TIME CAPSULE

Allow your children to decorate a box or container to use as your capsule to be added to each year. Pack your time capsule with mementos, pictures, and memories from the past year, and store it in a safe, safety deposit box at your bank, or secret place in your home. For a simple, space-saving idea, copy the "Snapshot of My Year" printable on the next page for each person in your family to complete and drop into your time capsule! For additional information on Time Capsules check out www.theidearoom.net/new-years-eve-time-capsule-printables and be sure to go to **www.myhelpclubformoms.com** for access to all of our printables.

PRAY TOGETHER FOR THE YEAR TO COME

Ask that the Lord would help each of your children to love Him and others more this year than ever before. Talk to them about seeking the Lord's will and plans for the coming year. Following Jesus daily is an exciting way of life!

CHOOSE A WORD TO REPRESENT THE UPCOMING YEAR

(This coming year could be the year of joy, faith, kindness, quietness, or thankfulness). Discuss the way your chosen word could play out in your children's daily life. Search your Bible or online concordance to find verses that apply. Make artwork, using markers, watercolor paints, or whatever you have on hand, depicting the theme for the year and how that word will be represented in your child's life.

HAVE A PARTY!

Use what you have on hand to make a fun, simple party! Be creative with party favors and props. Paper hats are fun and easy to make, and kids love to assemble and hang their own decorations. Have simple snacks and play board games or watch a favorite family movie. Your evening doesn't have to be complicated to create lasting memories, and family celebrations are truly building blocks for beautiful memories!

Snapshot
of my Year

Name:

Date:

Age: Height:

Favorite Trip:

Favorite Book:

Favorite Movie/TV Show:

Something I Learned:

Something New I Did:

Funniest Moment:

Favorite Memory:

An Oops:

My Goal for the New Year:

PICTURE OF ME

Help Club For Moms is a group of moms who seek to grow closer to God, closer to our families, and closer to each other. We believe prayer changes everything and God is big enough to help us raise the children with whom God has blessed us.

We focus on digging into God's Word, praying together, and encouraging one another! Through weekly "Mom Tips" and daily "Faith Filled Ideas," the Help Club for Moms helps women take what they are learning about the Lord and apply it to their daily journey as wives and mothers. Our goal is to spread the love of Jesus, inspire women to be the wives and mothers God created us to be and to impact eternity—One mama at a time!

Would you like to be a part of the movement?

Here's how you can get involved in the Help Club for Moms:

- Purchase our books on Amazon. We use 100% of the proceeds to fund our all-volunteer ministry. The titles are: *The Wise Woman Knows, The Wise Woman Loves, The Wise Woman Stays, The Wise Woman Abides, The Wise Woman Grows, The Wise Woman Enjoys, The 40-Day Joy Challenge for Moms, Holidays with the Help Club,* and *Help Club for Moms* published by Harvest House Publishers, coming April 2020.

- Pray for the ministry and the moms in our Help Club Community worldwide—for them to know the love of Jesus and create a Christ-Like atmosphere in their homes.

- Start a Help Club for Moms group at your local church or home. We can help you!

- We are always on the lookout for Titus 2 women who can help mentor our moms through social media and prayer.

- If you are an author, blogger, graphics artist, or social media guru, we need you and your talents at the Help Club!

- We are a 501(c)(3) and all volunteer ministry! Please go to www.helpclubformoms.com/donate/ to help us get God's Word into the hands of moms worldwide!

Questions? Email us at info@helpclubformoms.com.
You can find out more about Help Club for Moms at www.HelpClubForMoms.com and on Facebook and Instagram @HelpClubForMoms.

Church Resource Section

Moms encouraging moms to know the love of Christ

Dear Mom,

We are so very honored that you are journeying through this Bible study with us. What a gift you are to our ministry!

We wanted to make sure you knew that, built right into this book, is everything you need to start a "Help Club for Moms" group of your own! You can do it through your church or even as a small group in your home. Lives are changed when we read God's Word together and focus on becoming intentional moms and wives in community together! Doing a Help Club for Moms Bible Study is a chance for you and your friends to dive deeper into learning about God's design for motherhood. Plus, everything is more fun with friends!

It is so easy to lead a Help Club for Moms group. Each mom commits to following along in the Bible study. Then you meet at your home or church just twice per month to go over what you are learning and pray for one another. We even have a special group on Facebook dedicated to our Help Club for Moms Bible Study Leaders where we give you ideas with lesson plans for your group. Simply go to the *Help Club for Moms National Leaders Group* on Facebook, answer the questions and ask to join. It's that simple!

Doing life together as moms in a Christ-centered community draws us closer to Jesus and to each other while building friendship and connections that are sure to last a lifetime. What a great way to walk as moms, together arm-in-arm and with our eyes on Jesus, all the way until we get to heaven.

If you are interested in starting a Help Club for Moms group, either in your church or home, please email us at info@helpclubformoms.com. We would love to walk alongside you, give you helpful resources, and PRAY for you.

Blessings to you, mama!

Sincerely,

The Help Club for Moms Team

FAQ:
About Help Club For Moms

WHAT IS THE HELP CLUB FOR MOMS?

• Help Club for Moms is a community of moms encouraging moms to know the love of Christ. We value authentic, transparent relationships. Together, we study God's Word, pray, fellowship twice a month, and share practical "Mom Tips." All this to become the women, wives, and mothers God created us to be, and with the help of the Holy Spirit, bring up our children to do the same!

WHY CHOOSE HELP CLUB?

• Help Club For Moms offers a Christ-centered program focused on strengthening the church by strengthening moms, through teaching God's design for families and biblically based parenting.

• There is no fee for the program; the only cost is for the books which may be purchased on Amazon.

• The program is for moms of all ages. We love learning from each other in every stage of life!

• There are three simple, but deep, biblical studies per week, which teach and encourage moms, yet are still easy to accomplish. A must for today's busy mom!

• Help Club For Moms "Mom Tips" set us apart from other mom groups because every week, we offer eight practical, new ideas to strengthen and train women in their role as a wife, mother, and woman of God.

• Each mom in Help Club For Moms is partnered with another mom for prayer. Every week, these two moms pray for 10-15 minutes with one another over the phone, deepening their connection with God and each other. Prayer changes everything!

• Help Club For Moms brings godly community, support, fellowship, and friendship to families through the relationships formed between moms.

• HCFM's has three years of Christ-centered curriculum.

• HCFM has a strong presence on social media, which helps moms go deeper in the studies with other moms around the world.

WHAT ARE THE CORE VALUES OF HELP CLUB FOR MOMS?

• HCFM values authentic and transparent community between moms, deep growth in relationship with God, intentional Bible study, faithful prayer relationships between moms, and practical day-to-day ideas and tips for moms.

WHAT IS REQUIRED OF THE CHURCH?

• HCFM's partner churches should plan to help in two ways:

    1. Offer a meeting space for two hours/twice monthly

    2. Help with childcare for two hours/twice monthly

Hosting a HCFM's Meeting

WHAT DOES A TYPICAL HELP CLUB FOR MOMS MEETING LOOK LIKE?

• Hosting a Help Club meeting is easy and fun and is a great way to build community with the moms in your church or neighborhood. Below is a sample morning meeting schedule. (You could also host a "Help Club Mom's Night Out Potluck Dinner" instead of a daytime meeting for working moms or moms who want some time away while dad has the children.)

<u>SCHEDULE</u>

9:30-9:40 **Welcome, pray, and on time drawing with an inexpensive prize**

9:40-10:15 **Moms meet in groups to discuss current HCFM Bible study**
- Large groups: Moms sit around tables in small groups of 3-6 moms with a leader and possible co-leader to discuss content from the last two week's topic.
- Small groups or home study group: Moms sit in a circle as one big group to discuss content from the last two week's topic.

10:15-10:30 **Simple worship and announcements** (HCFM Spotify and Amazon Prime playlist and lyrics provided if desired)

10:30-10:35 **Book Review** (HCFM suggested book review provided if desired)

10:35-10:50 **Mom Tips in Action** (Invite one of your leaders/ helpers to spotlight a Mom Tip from this week's study and how she used it) Then, invite other moms from the group to share how they used a moms tip from the list or how they are planning to use one in the future. This is an important time for our moms to learn from each other.

10:50-11:15 **Devotion time**
There are two ways to facilitate a HCFM's devotion portion of the group: one led by a seasoned mom or one led by a young, peer aged mom.
- Both groups lead a discussion about the topic from the last two weeks of study by discussing Scripture and asking questions of the group about the topic. (Scripture applicable to the topic and "Questions to Ponder" are found in each study.) The leader shares her personal experiences as a fellow mom journeying on the road of motherhood. The leader may also choose to watch a portion of a Help Club for Moms "Mentoring Monday" video about the topic with the moms in her group.

11:15-11:25 **Moms pray with prayer partners**

11:25 **Pray and dismiss moms to pick up children**

All HCFM leaders have access to a private Facebook group (Help Club for Moms National Group Leaders) where they can access training videos, ask questions, and share ideas to help them host a successful group. **Questions? Email us at info@helpclubformoms.com.**

Book Recommendations

BOOKS FOR MOMS (NON-FICTION):

Parenting the Wholehearted Child
by Jeannie Cunnion

You and Me Forever by Francis and Lisa Chan
(marriage)

Daring Greatly by Brene Brown

The Ragamuffin Gospel by Brennan Manning

Love and Respect by Dr. Emmerson Eggerichs

Love and Respect in the family
by Dr. Emmerson Eggerichs

Mother and Son by Dr. Emmerson Eggerichs

The Circle Maker by Mark Batterson

The Power of a Praying Wife
by Stormie O' Martian

The Power of a Praying Parent
by Stormie O' Martian

The Read-Aloud Family by Sarah Mackenzie

BOOKS FOR MOMS (FICTION):

Mark of the Lion trilogy by Francine Rivers

Redeeming Love by Francine Rivers

Sarah's Key by Tatiana de Rosnay

The Help by Kathryn Stockett

BOOKS FOR KIDS:

Discipleship books:

The Picture Bible published by David C. Cook

The Jesus Storybook Bible by Sally Lloyd-Jones

The Action Bible by Sergio Cariello

Missionary Stories with the Millers
by Mildred A. Martin

Upper Elementary/Early Middle School (grades 4-7):

The Wingfeather Saga by Andrew Peterson

The Green Ember series by E.D. Smith

The Penderwicks series by Jeanne Birdsall

Lower Elementary (grades 2-3):

The Imagination Station by Marianne Hering

Greetings from Somewhere by Harper Paris

Dear Molly, Dear Olive by Megan Atwood

Early Readers (grades K-1):

Owl Diaries by Rebecca Elliot

I Can Read! Princess Parables by Jeanna Young

Jotham's Journey series

Little House on the Prairie by Laura Ingalls Wilder

The BFG by Roald Dahl

The Lion, The Witch, and the Wardrobe
by C.S. Lewis

Anne of Green Gables by Lucy Maud Montgomery

HOMESCHOOLING:

Teaching From Rest by Sarah Mackenzie

Educating the WholeHearted Child
by Clay Clarkson with Sally Clarkson

Seasons of a Mother's Heart by Sally Clarkson

Podcasts

PODCASTS FOR MOMS:

Don't Mom Alone

Coffee & Crumbs

Java with Juli

Cultivating the Lovely

Parenting Great Kids with Dr. Meg Meeker

Focus on the Family

The Messenger Podcast

Conversations with John and Lisa Bevere

I am Adamant Podcast by Lisa Bevere

Read Aloud Revival

Happy Hour with Jamie Ivey

PODCASTS FOR KIDS:

Stories Podcast

Storynory

Brains On! Science Podcast for Kids

Adventures in Odyssey

ONLINE SERMONS:

ChurchoftheHighlands.org

Theaterchurch.org

Worship Music

PANDORA HELP CLUB FOR MOMS STATION:

https://pdora.co/2KynyvV

SPOTIFY HELP CLUB FOR MOMS STATION:

https://spoti.fi/2lVBMbw

Made in the USA
San Bernardino, CA
09 November 2019